Broken Alabaster Jars

Portraits Of Women In Ministry

THE SALVATION ARMY

Anne Pickup

WINEPRESS WP PUBLISHING

Pickup, Anne, 1952–
Broken Alabaster Jars
Portraits of Women in Ministry
© 1998 by The General of The Salvation Army

Produced by:
The Salvation Army
Western Territory
30840 Hawthorne Blvd.
Rancho Palos Verdes, CA 90275

Published by:
WinePress Publishing
PO Box 1406
Mukilteo, WA 98275

Printed in the United States of America

ISBN 1-57921-084-8
Library of Congress Catalog Card Number: 97-62490

DEDICATION

To my mother,

Major Carol West Madsen,

whose life models a woman's ability to do many things
for God when abandoned love is the motive.

⚬

IN HONOR

of my husband and my champion,

Major Bill Pickup,

whose abandoned love for God
encouraged the best in me.

ACKNOWLEDGMENTS

A six-year dream has come true! It was my dream, but it would not have been fulfilled without the help of many friends:

- **Professor Karen Winslow**: who ignited a desire to investigate female leadership throughout the church's history, which correspondingly led to my deeper understanding of biblical interpretation.
- **Bill Pickup**: champion of my dream, whose last words of instruction were, "Get your book published, whatever it takes."
- **Bill** and **Linda**: my children, who have had to live with a dream that wasn't theirs, turning down stereos, giving me study time, and eating fast-food hamburgers.
- **Bay Area Book Group**: Jim Black, Marion Black, Cyndi Lycan, Scott Lycan, Wendy Webster, Tim Webster, and Bill—my encouragers, whose brutal honesty taught me much.
- **Sue Schumann**: friend, encourager, editor, and project manager.

- **Deborah Flagg**: an excellent writer who also edits.
- **Sr. Major Helena Sainsbury**: a magnificent woman in my life, who is both a great aunt and practical supporter.
- **Literary Council of the Western Territory**: who endorsed the dream and made it come true.
- GOD: the Giver of Dreams, . . . what's next?

CONTENTS

FOREWORD

   One of the greatest legacies from Catherine and William Booth to the church was that of women in ministry. Opening the doors of ministry to women as well as to men in the Christian Mission and later in The Salvation Army meant being faithful to the clear biblical witness of both daughters and sons preaching the good news. The history of The Salvation Army has amply proved the wisdom of this theological position as untold thousands of women have followed the path of Catherine Booth and used their many gifts for the sake of the kingdom of God.

   Major Anne Pickup has provided an immeasurable service to the Army and the wider Christian community by reminding us of the biblical and historic foundations of our understanding of women in ministry. She has skillfully woven the stories of women from the Bible and the history of the church with those of women in the history of the Army, and in doing so has demonstrated her own delight in those narratives. The lives of many women unfold in the text, and Anne Pickup has treated those lives with the attention and the dignity they deserve. She shows the pathos and the drama as well as the humor and the glory of their paths of service. The humanity of the women she has chosen shines through the text, which makes this book such interesting reading.

One of the most significant aspects of this book for Salvationists is the Salvation Army women she has chosen to portray. In many cases her examples are of women serving in humble, and often difficult, circumstances—a reminder to us all that many of the greatest women we have known have not been the famous but those who serve the Lord Jesus Christ in obscurity. Nevertheless, their service for Christ and his kingdom are equally acceptable to God, and in this we all rejoice.

This book should be read by men as well as women because it is a constant and faithful reminder of our shared humanity in Jesus Christ as well as our shared ministry for his sake. Anne Pickup has well dedicated this book to her mother, and written it in honor of her husband and my lifelong friend, Bill. In doing so Anne has reminded us at the outset of the book of her own and Bill's example of shared ministry, where gifts and abilities are used without reserve and where such gifts are encouraged in the other. And so, Major Anne Pickup brings to this book her own example of strength and courage in the midst of life's difficulties, and yet moves the readers on to see the triumph of lives well lived and commitments well kept in the service of the Lord.

I commend this work to all who will read this book. In doing so you will begin a journey commencing with the pages of the Bible and the history of the church and ending with the history of The Salvation Army, which continues to attempt to be faithful to the biblical promise that "Your sons and your daughters shall prophesy" (Acts 2:17). You will rejoice as I have done in the witness of these daughters of the church. You will bless God for giving them opportunities for many ministries, and you will thank them for being faithful to the God of their salvation.

Dr. Roger J. Green
Professor and Chair of Biblical
and Theological Studies
Terrelle B. Crum Chair of Humanities
Gordon College
Wenham, Massachusetts

INTRODUCTION

This is a book about women worth knowing and remembering.

A few years ago, when completing my degree in religious history, I took a class on women in the church. As we
studied the consistent and valuable contribution of women
throughout church history, I was continually frustrated by
the glaring absence of Salvationist women in the textbooks.
My mind overflowed with images of wonderful female servants whose deeds were unrecorded and whose lives were
forgotten.

The Salvation Army, from its founding in 1865, gave
equal rights to women. Catherine Booth, co-founder with
her husband, William, had studied Scripture and discovered the freedom Jesus granted to women in the first-century church. In contrast to other denominations, The Salvation Army held an egalitarian view of women in ministry
and leadership. From its beginnings in London, England,
The Salvation Army has offered ordination and an open
door of service to women. I knew this, but it seemed hardly
anyone else did.

This was an omission of staggering magnitude. Someone should do something about it! Someone should write a book and tell the world about this great army of God and the opportunities it offers women. To honor the memory of countless female soldiers, someone ought to record the beautiful deeds they have accomplished and tell how the fragrance of their ministry has permeated the world.

That someone became me. While I watched a gorgeous sunset create swirls of orange and pink that filled the sky over Puget Sound in Seattle, Washington, God placed a dream in my heart.

Since I was the one who discovered this glaring omission, I must be the person to set the record straight. I must find the material and make it available. These loving acts of Salvationist women must be recorded and remembered.

With the goal embraced, I set out to find the women whose stories must be told and whose lives should be kept alive in our memory. I sent questionnaires to five hundred Salvationists and asked, "Who are the women who have impacted your life, other people's lives, corps [churches], and communities around the United States?"

More than two hundred names were submitted. I read the tributes, absorbing the impact of their ministry. I felt as if I were surrounded by the cloud of witnesses spoken of in Hebrews 12! These were heroines of the faith who had served as laity and officers since World War II, creating the most recent chapter in the history of The Salvation Army in the United States. These women of God had formed the army in which I now serve. These were the women who, through acts of abandoned love, have ministered to Jesus himself. Their lives are worth remembering.

There is not enough room to tell two hundred stories! As I pored over the list of names, a few special women rose to the top because of their particular leadership and service. I traveled around the United States to meet and interview them and to hear their stories firsthand.

What an experience! As these women told their stories, I was blessed. Their lives clearly testified to what God can do with a person who gives her dearest and best. They told me of their calling to ministry. They told me of their joy in service. They shared the difficulties life had brought them. We laughed and cried together. Through their words I heard their love for God and saw how this foundation gave them the courage to be exactly who God created them to be. God's clear calling and equipping gave them strength to remain faithful in the work he appointed them to do, even when criticized.

Their stories clarified and defined my story, and God used their lives to confirm my calling. Their satisfaction with God's movement in their lives brought new contentment to my life. Their excitement in service, even when laced with struggles, reminded me that joy comes through obedience. Each accepted herself just as God created her. Each acknowledged both strengths and limitations. These wonderful stories of women who performed memorable acts of love to Jesus demand a response. My response was to thank God for who I am and then to find my place in the Body of Christ.

I hope that from these stories you, too, will be reminded that God created men and women to be in partnership in life and in service. I pray that as you learn of the beautiful, extravagant, loving deeds of these women, your relationship with Christ will be strengthened and you will be encouraged to create fragrant memories in the kingdom of God through your life.

As a gift of abandoned love for Jesus, I tell these stories, hoping to hear Jesus say, as paraphrased by Eugene Peterson in *The Message,* "She has done something wonderfully significant."

CHAPTER ONE

Broken Jars

She Did What She Could

(Mark 14)

"Oh, what endears the Christian religion to my heart is what it has done, and is destined to do, for my own sex."
—*Catherine Booth*

Jesus relaxed at the dinner table, surrounded by an odd assortment of people. Peter, his brother Andrew, and James and his brother John—men who had left home and family to follow this one claiming to be the Messiah—reclined on mats around this u-shaped, ground level table. With them were Judas Iscariot, Philip, Thomas, James of Alphaeus, Thaddaeus, and Bartholomew, men who left careers to wander Israel behind an itinerant preacher. Also in the company were Simon, a zealot, and Matthew, a tax collector, men who were finding new ways to direct their passions and skills through the teaching of Jesus.

And there were women! At the table with Jesus were the three Marys—Jesus' mother, Mary; Mary Magdalene; and Mary the mother of James and Joses. Also present were women of wealth—Joanna, Suzanna, and Salome. These women dining with Jesus had been in the entourage of disciples traveling around Galilee.

Simon the Leper hosted this event. Of course, he was no longer a leper, as lepers live with their dreaded disease outside of normal society. Jesus had healed Simon, but as a witness to this healing grace, he chose to keep the stigma of a leper.

The hungry crowd welcomed the food, but exhaustion made it hard for them to eat. They could no longer tell if their emptiness came from hunger or fatigue. Each needed refreshment and rest. It had been a hectic and emotional three days.

Following the Sabbath, on the first day of the week, Jesus had entered Jerusalem on the back of a donkey. Crowds waved palm branches and cried, "Hosanna! Blessed is he who comes in the name of the Lord!" The announcement marked the arrival of a king—at least to some. After this very high moment, Jesus and his followers entered the Temple to experience a profound low.

Jesus was appalled at what he saw! A place of prayer and communing with God had become the profit-making business of religion. He cried out in anguish, turned over tables, and brashly confronted the selfish motives of the merchants. He was not liked. Yet he spoke with such authority that they couldn't help but listen. Many responded to the truth of his words, but others, threatened by the disturbance, sought ways to entrap and get rid of him.

Disregarding the threat to his life, Jesus went to the Temple daily to pray and to teach. In contrast to more relaxed times on the calm shores of the Sea of Galilee, his teaching had grown in intensity. His words were now powerful, pulsating with urgency, and filled with the passion of one who knows he is running out of time.

And so the quiet dinner at Simon's house in Bethany was a welcome change. Soft conversations accompanied the delicious food that was served in abundance. But Passover was just two days away, and in the midst of this subdued gathering Jesus began saying some frightening things, such as "I will be arrested," and "I will be killed." Oh, for just one stress-free evening!

Unnamed Woman

Having neither name nor introduction, a woman entered quietly. At first only Jesus noticed her, but soon every eye focused on this unannounced guest. She carried an alabaster jar, its translucent quality embracing the glow from the candles. Jesus adjusted his posture to allow her to come near. She knelt in front of him, broke the beautiful jar, and—without speaking a word—eagerly poured its expensive contents over Jesus' head. She tenderly smoothed the ointment onto his hair and face by gentle strokes of her hands. As the perfumed ointment flowed over his body, so her hands flowed in slow, soft movements. She anointed Jesus from head to toe. The strong fragrance filled the room.

As the fragrance intensified, so did the tension. Who was this woman? Who did she think she was, barging in on this private dinner, violating the personal space of one so revered? Judas Iscariot was outraged at the wasteful extravagance of this woman. The value of the perfume equaled a year's salary—enough to feed hundreds, maybe thousands, of hungry people. Jesus, do something, say something!

"Leave her alone," said Jesus. "She has done a beautiful thing to me. The poor you will always have with you, and you can help them any time you want. But you will not always have me. She did what she could. She poured perfume on my body beforehand to prepare for my burial."

Prompted by God and filled with love for Jesus, this woman performed an act of extravagant love. She gave herself in ministry to Jesus by doing what she could, where she was. Onlookers criticized her activity as wasteful, objectionable, and even outrageous. Jesus called it beautiful.

Serving Jesus cost her dearly. Her actions flowed from who she was and what she had to offer, and love was her only motive. Driven to minister by selfless abandonment, she found that her deed was both acceptable and honorable to Jesus. He said, "I tell you the truth, wherever this gospel is preached throughout the world, what she has done will also be told in memory of her."

Were the actions of this woman and their meaning to the kingdom of God an anomaly? Did Jesus allow her to violate a cultural norm that held to "men only" in ministry? Was this a fluke, a once-in-a-lifetime abnormality fitting only to this moment in time?

No! There is a continuing witness of women in Scripture and church history displaying the acceptable, honorable ministries of women to the kingdom of God. From the Old Testament period until this very day God has used, involved, and valued the contributions of female saints. Ministry, flowing from selfless abandonment—acts of extravagant love and worthy service—have been a calling for women as well as for men.

Women have a rich heritage in the kingdom of God. The Bible tells the stories of many women who were crucial to the fulfillment of prophecy and important in representing a God of love and grace to the world. At Pentecost, the birth of the Christian church, women were not only present but filled with the power and giftedness of the Holy Spirit. As the church expanded throughout the world, women continued to play vital roles through ever-growing expressions of ministry.

The richness added to the kingdom of God through the contributions of female saints will not be fully known until we reach heaven. Until that great day we must open our eyes to recognize and honor, as Jesus did, the blessed ministries of women.

Catherine Booth

There are no richer, more honorable ministries found than those of the women in The Salvation Army. Since its founding in 1865, The Salvation Army has not only honored, but depended on, the service of women to the cause of Christ. William Booth, co-founder and first General, once said, "Some of my best men are women." This reality came to the general through the continuing, faithful witness of his wife, Catherine. She had had her own moment of "breaking the alabaster jar." She had stepped out in abandoned love on a Pentecost Sunday at the Methodist New Connexion Bethesda Chapel in Gateshead, England.

Before rising to public ministry herself, Catherine Booth defended the right of a woman to do so. Her defense, written in 1859 in the form of a pamphlet entitled *Female Ministry: Or Women's Right to Preach the Gospel*, was not for herself but advocated an American holiness preacher, Phoebe Palmer.

On a four-year speaking tour of England with her husband, Phoebe was soundly criticized by the Reverend Arthur Augustus Rees for her part in the Newcastle Revival. Even though the two women had not met, Catherine was incensed by Reverend Rees's remarks against Phoebe and felt for the sake of the kingdom of God a positive statement should be made.

Catherine argued against a common misconception that "woman had a fiber more in her heart and a cell less in her brain." She knew that the lack of intelligence and skill found in women was better blamed on a lack of training and education. But her greater defense came from the Bible. Catherine believed that women were not only given the right of ministry, but were called to ministry—not in spite of Scripture but because of it! Of the call to freedom in Christ stated in Galatians 3:28, Catherine wrote, "If this passage does not teach that in the privileges, duties, and responsibilities of Christ's kingdom, all differences of nation, caste, and sex are abolished, we should like to know what it does teach, and wherefore it was written."

Her final defense from Scripture, found in Acts 2, rested on the record of events at Pentecost, fifty days after Jesus' death. The apostle Peter claimed this day of wonder as the fulfillment of Joel 2, the coming of the promised Holy Spirit. Catherine reminded her readers that the Spirit fell on all in that room, "the sons and daughters," thus bringing to rest all questions regarding the equality of men and women in regard to salvation *and* ministry.

Still, Catherine hadn't broken her alabaster jar . . . until another Pentecost Sunday in 1860. Sitting in Bethesda Chapel with about a thousand people, Catherine listened as her husband, William, concluded his sermon. She then rose to her feet and walked toward the podium. William couldn't imagine what her purpose was except that maybe something awful had happened. He stepped down and asked Catherine, "What is the matter, my dear?"

She simply replied, "I want to say a word."

His shocked response to the congregation was only, "My dear wife wants to say a word." And he sat down.

Catherine broke her alabaster jar through confession: "I dare say many of you have been looking upon me as a very devoted woman, and one who has been living faithfully to God, but I have come to know that I have been living in disobedience, and to that extent I have brought darkness and leanness into my soul, but I promised the Lord three or four months ago, and I dare not disobey. I have come to tell you this, and to promise the Lord that I will be obedient to the heavenly vision."

The heavenly vision was her active participation in ministry through preaching, teaching, visiting, and serving— whatever the Lord asked. It was the pouring out of her very self. This moment of complete, abandoned love made her forever available to fulfill the words of Jesus: "She did what she could."

The fragrance of that outpouring permeated The Salvation Army. From its inception in 1865, The Salvation Army has held to an equality of women and men in ministry. This is an organizational premise based on scriptural mandates.

Every day, throughout the United States, thousands of Salvationist women serve Jesus through acts of abandoned love. God honors them all, but only a few can be recorded here.

They are remembered in the context of their sisters of earlier centuries who went before them in service, modeling what can be done for Jesus when listening to the leading of God, not the opinions of people. Godly women of yesterday, placed side by side with godly women of today, model the continuing witness of female saints, each performing beautiful acts motivated by abandoned love.

CHAPTER TWO

EVANGELISTS

He Sets the Captive Free

"His Spirit, given equally to woman as to man, makes itself heard within us. We know that, unless we have his Spirit, we are none of his, and if we have his Spirit, its fruits will not be different in us to those in our brethren."

—*Emma Moss Booth-Tucker*

Clang! The prison doors closed behind me in the Winnebago County Jail in Rockford, Illinois.

I arrived on a cold, rainy Sunday in November. All my belongings were taken from me—briefcase, wallet, hairbrush, pens—everything! Certified as free of contraband, I was led through a door and up a flight of stairs. At the top of the stairs stood a classic iron prison gate. The matron unlocked the iron gate and ushered me in. It automatically closed and locked behind us. We stood in a small enclosure waiting for a solid metal door to be opened from the other side. Another uniformed matron opened the heavy door and escorted me through one final locked metal door. Passing through this door, I was truly a captive.

I stood in an overcrowded room called a *tier*. It had been built to hold sixteen women, but thirty-two women, wearing orange cotton jumpsuits, now occupied this small space. Standing in the middle of the tier, I saw everything—eight bunk beds, numerous floormats, three tables bolted to the floor with attached seats, a TV mounted on the wall, and a corner door that led to a bathroom with two toilets and two showers. Not a pleasant place. Less pleasant in the stifling, stale heat! This crowded, depressing place was filled with broken women whom society abhorred and didn't want to see.

At least I was there voluntarily. I had come with a group of women from The Salvation Army Rockford Temple Corps for their monthly chapel service. The message of hope delivered by these ladies is always the same. "Despite your physical circumstances, Jesus sets the captive free."

The leader was Envoy Shirley Lindstrom Kerestesi, a woman in her late fifties with a face showing years of hard living, framed by bouffant bleached-blonde hair and punctuated with a great smile!

"The girls look forward to our coming," she grinned.

Shirley introduced me to every orange-clad woman. She called them by name and greeted them with a huge hug. "I love these girls like my own daughters. I understand exactly what they are thinking and going through."

Shirley understands because she too has worn the orange jumpsuit of an inmate. Once she was locked behind these prison doors, held captive by the law but more so by her own bitterness and anger. One day, behind locked doors, she experienced a miraculous encounter with Jesus Christ. At that moment she was set free.

Jesus began his ministry when he was thirty years old. From the beginning he declared his mission: "to bind up the brokenhearted, to proclaim freedom for the captives, and to release from darkness the prisoners."

People who were imprisoned by low self-esteem, bound in anger, and chained hopelessly to despair could be set free by the love, peace, and joy Jesus offered. And, once free, the former prisoners couldn't help but share the good news. These people became effective evangelists for the gospel. These converts, both women and men, became God's most valuable participants in helping others find freedom in Christ.

Time has not changed this truth. The most freeing experience is when we come face to face with Jesus, confess our sin, and receive his forgiveness. The most powerful testimonies are from those who have been forgiven much. Two women of different eras, imprisoned by their destructive behaviors, encountered Christ and found freedom. Both became effective evangelists in their communities. One met Jesus at a well.

The Samaritan Woman (circa A.D. 29)
It was a blistering, hot day, not ideal for traveling the long, dry miles from Jerusalem to Capernaum in Galilee. But today Jesus told the disciples they were going home. The usual route led inland along the Jordan River, but Jesus insisted on traveling directly north, through the region of Samaria.

Yes, it was a shorter route, but the Samaritans were defiled people. They were Jews who had intermarried and created a self-styled religion. They had lost the purity of their Jewishness and were hatefully avoided.

"I live in Sycar in the region of Samaria," said the Samaritan woman. She was a woman with a past, and it showed. She had a rugged face and a sturdy body.

While respectable women wore their hair bound and covered, her hair, tinted an unnatural color, flowed wildly, and her reputation was consistent with her hairstyle.

Drawing the daily water supply was a woman's job. "Women go as a group in the cool morning hours to get their water from Jacob's well. I was never invited to join them. I had been married too many times, I guess. If they only knew why."

As a child this Samaritan woman had had a terrible experience with a man. Since then she seemed to attach herself to abusive men. "Some were physically abusive, and all my husbands were verbally abusive. You see, women are just property to be owned, items to be used. Love, honor, value, and esteem were unfamiliar ideas to me. Yes, I have been married five times and was living with a man. Why marry again? If this one was mean, at least I could leave or make him leave."

This lifestyle seemed to work for her, but she suffered times of unbearable loneliness. Some days the snide remarks pierced her heart. She had few friends. Life droned on in a dreary ordinariness.

"It was a typical day, except it seemed warmer than usual. Once the others had drawn their water, I made my way to Jacob's well. A man was sitting there, obviously a Jew. I was shocked to see him in Samaria and completely surprised when he spoke to me.

"He asked for a drink of water." She still seemed stunned. "And then he went on about always being thirsty and living water and, well, I don't know. Maybe the heat had him half out of his mind. Maybe he knew of a better well, one I could go to and avoid the sneers and stares of people."

The Samaritan woman's eyes were wide as saucers. "Then he said, 'Go get your husband!' I didn't know what to say. My first husband? My fifth husband? The man I was living with? Was he from the Temple? Was he an official from Sycar looking for a way to run me off?"

She didn't know him. He wasn't from Sycar. She knew all the men in town, and he was definitely a stranger—and a Jew. He then told her all about her ruined past. The hurts. The abuse. The rejection. He explained her personal imprisonment and despair perfectly.

With unwitting insight, she said, "I don't know much. I'm not religious, but I do know everybody is waiting for some Savior they call Messiah. They say we will know it is him because he will know all about us. You don't know me, but you know all about me. Are you the one everybody has been waiting for?"

"Yes, I am," was Jesus' uncomplicated reply.

They stood there face to face, her heart throbbing with a mixture of fear and excitement. He was calm and kind. Her hard, cold heart seemed to be melting within her into something soft and warm. Years of anger were replaced with forgiveness. Wounds of rejection were healed. Hatred was turned to love. Her voice softened. Her clenched fist released. Her face lit up. All the chains that had bound her for years were broken, and she was set free.

"I raced into the city with speed I hadn't experienced in years. The people probably thought I had snapped. I called out, begging them to listen to me. 'Just give me a minute of your time!'" Her words tumbled out quickly in a torrent.

"Groups of people gathered around me, and I told them about Jesus. Then I moved to another group and told them the same thing. They were intrigued, and some followed me out to the well to see this man."

It wasn't just her words. Without realizing it, the woman's whole demeanor had changed. Her sentences weren't filled with obscenities. A peaceful joy radiated from her face. This woman had experienced something. It was noticeable and worth investigating.

Jesus stayed for two days in Sycar.

"I kept bringing more people to Jesus. I felt so different. So free. So alive. I wanted everyone to feel what I felt."

Still as excited as if it were yesterday, she continued, "Doors of emotions that had been closed for so long were opening. Chains that bound my mind were broken. Relationships were mended. Just when I thought it was impossible, I felt hope again. My greatest joy was seeing it happen in other people. Even people I thought had no problems were being set free from things that imprisoned them. We were one happy bunch of people! We were a perfect example of captive people experiencing the joy of being set free."

An outcast woman of Samaria, imprisoned by the pains of life, encountered Jesus Christ. She was a captive set free. She became Sycar's greatest evangelist. God used her testimony to draw others to himself. We read her story in the New Testament and remember.

But a similar story is found in twentieth-century Rockford, Illinois. This story is told in memory of her.

Envoy Shirley Lindstrom Kerestesi

Pacing back and forth like a caged lion—banging the walls, rattling the bars, and yelling a steady stream of obscenities—Shirley Lindstrom at forty-three years of age found herself behind prison doors. Arrested for attempted murder, she was now locked in a cell at the Winnebago County Jail in Rockford, Illinois. How had she gotten into such a mess?

Shirley's second marriage was into its third year—three years of continual verbal abuse by an alcoholic husband. According to her husband, Shirley did everything wrong. She had caused all their problems. She was a failure, a disaster, and the worst thing that ever happened to anybody. After three years of listening to this, Shirley began to believe it.

On a hot day in August, Shirley's husband once again ranted and raved about all her flaws. This time it went beyond verbal abuse. Shirley ended up in the hospital, battered and bruised. Lying in her hospital bed, she made a tearful call to a male friend, pleading, "You have to help me!" He promised to "take care of things." No one was hired; no money passed hands, but it was a contract for murder.

A few weeks later, the friend arrived at Shirley's home in a drunken stupor with a loaded gun. He fired several times, but only one bullet grazed her husband's arm. Police arrested Shirley for attempted murder and took her to jail.

Her life was a mess. Her abusive husband was alive and at home while she was in prison. Shame overwhelmed her. What would her two daughters think? Her granddaughter? The rest of her family? A failure and an embarrassment, Shirley decided life was not worth living.

Finding a scrap of paper and a small pencil, Shirley wrote a suicide note to her two daughters. She loved them, but not life. They would be better off without her. Shirley decided to wait until after dinner when the jail was quiet and the matrons stayed away to let the inmates sleep. She had a sharp object, and during the quiet night hours she would end it all by slitting her wrists.

The waiting was unbearable. Reviewing her life, looking at her present misery, and ranting at being locked up, Shirley spewed filthy, vile words. A woman in the next cell, disturbed by the commotion, suggested she might benefit from a visit to the chaplain.

"I didn't know what a chaplain was, but that woman said I could get out from behind the bars," Shirley explained. A matron took her to the chaplain's office.

"The chaplain was a man!" she discovered, amazed. He greeted Shirley with a warm handshake and a kind smile.

Shirley remembers, "I hated this guy from the very beginning because he had this stupid grin on his face. I just wanted to knock it off! I didn't see anything so funny."

Chaplain Bill Bartholomew asked a few questions. One plunged her into a rage. "What do you think about God, Shirley?"

She jumped up, threw his papers, banged his desk, and pelted him with unbelievable words. Her uncontrollable outburst lasted forty-five minutes with Shirley hardly drawing a breath. Years of anger exploded. Her childhood in Catholic schools had introduced her to a God of punishment and judgment. A priest had molested her. No one, not even her mother, believed her tearful story about the priest. Religion, church, and God meant only pain and trouble.

Finally, the chaplain said it was his turn. He had listened to Shirley's view of God, and now it was her turn to listen to his. His God, he explained, is kind and loving and respects the free will he gives his creation.

Shirley responded, "You're a liar! Scripture is just black words on white paper. They're all lies, and you're being paid to tell me lies." Chaplain Bill gave Shirley a Bible so she could read along with him. But Shirley kept it closed and placed it on her lap. "I had never touched a Bible in my entire life," she said. "It sat there on my lap and sent a warm feeling through my body."

The matron appeared at the door. Her time was up, the visit over. Shirley remembers turning and looking at the chaplain as she left. "He did one more stupid thing with his usual stupid grin. He gave me a pencil and paper and said I should write down some things to talk about at our next visit.

"I was flabbergasted! I asked, 'You want to talk to me again? After I cussed at you and messed up your stuff? You want to talk to me again?'

"He answered quietly, 'Yes, I do.'

"I remember walking out of his door and thinking, *Wow! You must get paid big bucks to do what you do! If I get out of the trouble I'm in, I'm going to be one of the things you are.*"

Locked again in her cell, she refused dinner and lay down on the floor. It was 4:20 P.M. Shirley Lindstrom was held captive not just by the law, but by her wounded past. A glimmer of hope began to shine in her desperate moment. Maybe she could get out of this mess and get into a lucrative job like Chaplain Bill Bartholomew!

Stretched out on the floor, Shirley opened the Bible to see what this strange, warming book was all about. She opened first to the Book of Job.

Oh here it is! she thought. *This must be about the job this man has. If I read this, I'll know how to get this job. I can learn about being a chaplain and earn big bucks!*

As she read, she realized it was the story of a man named Job (pronounced "Jobe" but still "job" to her!). She couldn't believe the calamities that fell on this man!

She found herself yelling, "Job, you are so stupid! God hasn't done half the things to me that he's done to you, and he's not doing any more because I'm killing myself tonight. But you! Look what he's done to you. He's taken everything from you. He took your land, your animals, your family. All this suffering!"

Then Shirley saw that no matter what happened, Job never cursed God! She found this simply amazing. At first she thought he was just stupid! But then she realized he had been a man of great wealth, and wealthy people aren't usually stupid. She had to read on.

"I read the Book of Acts next, then John. I started reading about a man named Jesus Christ. The only Jesus Christ I knew was in cursing. But this was a man who died out of love, and I started seeing this kind, loving God the chaplain told me about."

Hooked on the book, Shirley did what a lot of readers do—she skipped to the end to see what happens. "I've got to read the end of the book because if I don't like how a book ends, I don't finish reading it."

She turned to the Book of Revelation. "It started out with streets of gold, rubies, and diamonds—my kind of book! Big bucks, no whammies! And there was excitement. I love excitement!"

Reading through Revelation was fun, so she decided to do it again to see if she had missed anything! During the second reading a verse seemed to rise from the page. "I read Revelation 3:20 where Jesus says, 'I stand and knock at the door. If you will open the door and let me in, I will come.'"

That warm feeling was returning. "I didn't know what that meant. I really didn't. Something inside told me I needed something I didn't have. I got on my knees on the jail floor, and there—for the first time in my life—I prayed.

"I really didn't know how to pray, and I had this struggle going on inside, but I cried out to God. If there really is a man named Jesus, then prove it to me!

"I prayed and I prayed, and I sobbed and I sobbed! I asked God to forgive me. I asked him to forgive anyone who had ever hurt me, including my husband and the priest."

The matron appeared again at 5:20 A.M. Shirley had been reading the Bible and praying for thirteen hours. The warm feeling was constant now, but new feelings also appeared. Clean feelings. Feelings of joy.

Maybe she didn't know how to pray, but when it was all over—even though she was locked in jail—she was free within. Shirley says, "For the first time in my life, I had joy in my heart."

Shirley had never felt joy, love, or inner peace in forty-three years. Now these feelings enveloped her. She loved it, but feared she would lose it. She went to see the chaplain.

"It took the chaplain nine sessions, seventy-two hours in all, to convince me that I could lie down and go to sleep, and when I woke up I would still have that feeling. I thought once I lay down and went to sleep, I would feel the same old way again. I was afraid. I didn't want that feeling to ever leave me. But I was getting tired!"

While Shirley was still in the county jail, The Salvation Army made its monthly Sunday visit. Shirley met Corps Sergeant Major Norma Baker. They rejoiced together!

Released on bond to a shelter for abused women, Shirley went to church at The Salvation Army. She had fourteen months of freedom while awaiting trial for attempted murder. During those months, she faithfully attended the corps; Chaplain Bill discipled her; and she grew in her relationship with Jesus.

At her trial Shirley was convicted of attempted murder and sentenced to six years in Dwight State Penitentiary, a maximum security prison. It was 138 miles from Rockford to the prison, and Shirley prayed all the way. She said, "Jesus, you have to go in this prison with me. You have to come through those gates and put your hand on my shoulder. Without you, I'm not going to make it."

He did! Incarceration creates no barriers for God. Shirley served three of the six years, getting time off for good behavior. While in prison she completed an AA degree. She wrote a monthly religious column for the prison newspaper and participated in a Bible study.

Chaplain Bill drove her home to Rockford on the day of her release. It was the fall, and she got a job at The Salvation Army helping with the Christmas effort. After Christmas, she became the corps office secretary. Then she became the director of the Community Youth Center. At the Youth Center, The Salvation Army officer noticed Shirley's "streetwise" skills and her ease with gang members.

In May 1989, Shirley became an envoy in The Salvation Army, serving as chaplain to the county jails and state prisons of northern Illinois. Fourteen years have passed since her arrest. Now *she* carries the keys to the iron gates at Winnebago County Jail. Now *she* is the chaplain. She doesn't get paid "big bucks," but she does experience big thrills by telling women and men about a kind, loving God. Shirley is an enthusiastic, loving evangelist in overcrowded tiers and cells of hurting people.

Once a loud, angry woman consumed with hate, Shirley is now filled with love. "When I got up off the floor that morning fourteen years ago, God filled my heart with love. Before I used to love hurting people. I used to love fights. I got high on blood! Now I am filled with love for all people."

As a member of the Hell's Henchmen gang, Shirley cared for only herself. Now she moves graciously and kindly among the incarcerated of Illinois. "God has given me the gift of compassion."

Her life is a testament to the promise of Romans 8:28. God is capable of taking all the parts of our lives, even the ugly and painful, and weaving them into a thing of beauty.

She was changed by a simple verse, Revelation 3:20. "Listen! I am standing at the door, knocking; if you hear my voice and open the door, I will come in to you and eat with you, and you with me." Now Shirley shares this verse at every opportunity. Her evangelistic message and ministry flow from personal experience.

"Prison doors mean nothing to God. The only door that matters is your heart's door. Only we can open that door. If we do, we will be free! And we will get joy that never goes away!"

God has blessed Envoy Shirley Lindstrom's evangelistic ministry. She has brought countless convicts and criminals, broken men and women, to Jesus. "Accepting Jesus, opening the heart door, and being set free from sin—that's what it's all about." Some converts have joined The Salvation Army. Many have returned to their home churches as regenerated people.

But evangelism isn't 100 percent successful! Shirley's heart has grieved many times for lost souls. After she's given all of her love and energy, some inmates will reject Jesus. Even after weeks and months of discipling, someone will fall into sin again. At these times Shirley says, "I cry. I just put my head in my arms and cry. I hurt for them because they don't understand they can feel like I feel. Then I hurt for myself because I feel inadequate. I figure I could have done something that I didn't. I feel that I somehow let them down."

God has a way of encouraging us in our despairing moments. For Shirley it often comes in the form of a letter. "I'll come to the office, and there will be a letter from an inmate thanking me for something I did or for showing them the real God. Then it's worth it all!"

This story has a postscript. First, on July 19, 1996, Shirley married Joseph Gabriel Kerestesi, also an ex-offender saved by grace. With the typical joy of a new bride, Shirley says, "For the first time in my entire life, I know and experience the full meaning of 'wedded bliss.' Joseph and I are best friends, partners, and lovers."

Second, Shirley has asked the governor of Illinois for a pardon. Why, after turning her life around and living as a productive citizen, would she seek a pardon?

She explains, "My life has been transformed, and I'd like to do something that will show this complete change. I am not the Shirley who committed the offense on record.

Plus, Jesus said we should ask for forgiveness. So I'm asking publicly to be forgiven."

If the governor responds favorably, what a business card Shirley can have printed!

Envoy Shirley
Lindstrom Kerestesi

Salvation Army Chaplain

"Twice Pardoned"
Revelation 3:20

CHAPTER THREE

DEACONS

Liberty to Serve

"Paul, who has been called 'the great silencer' so far as woman's public ministry is concerned, nevertheless entrusted women with some of the most difficult and delicate work of the infant churches."

—*Bramwell Booth*

"Some of my best men are women!" exclaimed William Booth, co-founder and first general of The Salvation Army. It was a compliment to the many women who were serving faithfully and successfully in the burgeoning movement, but it was also a rebuttal to critics of the Army's use of women in ministry.

Involvement of women in church leadership and government has been hotly debated since the Day of Pentecost, the birth of the Christian church. The debate continues to this day. Many have limited the roles and spheres of leadership for women, while others have pleaded for liberty.

The biblical record shows a steady stream of female involvement in ancient Israel in Jesus' ministry and the early Christian church. In Scripture we see example after example of women at work in the plans and purposes of God.

Following Pentecost, the newborn church grew rapidly. Within a few years, congregations were active in all parts of the Roman Empire. As the church grew in scope, numbers, and ministry, more and more people were needed to carry out its programs and purposes. This growth resulted in the establishment of many church offices, including the role of *deacon*.

The deacon was a servant of the church. Deacons preached and served in various ways within the Body of Christ. Their function was as diverse as the need and as flexible as the person serving in the situation. Women, as well as men, were deacons. The term *deaconess*, a feminine form of the word, is not found in the Bible. The medieval church created the word in an attempt to separate female roles from male roles. This gender difference is not biblical and does not reflect the reality that women and men served together in the early church. The one who did the job, gave the leadership, and provided the service was determined by availability, skill, and spiritual maturity—not gender.

The Salvation Army was born in England at the height of the Industrial Revolution of the nineteenth century, an era in which a woman's role in both the church and society was narrowly defined. Catherine and William Booth, students of the early Christian church, saw not only the need for new methodology in preaching the gospel but a renewed vision and definition of the priesthood of all believers.

If the church were to fulfill its mission on earth, it would take everybody—women and men—to lead and serve. The

Salvation Army restored the biblical birthright of women, giving to them the position of deacon with the fullest and most liberal definition of the term.

One hundred and thirty years of ministry have produced countless female Salvationist deacons (local officers) who minister and are faithful servants of the church. Thousands upon thousands of lives have been touched through them. By the hands and hearts of women, the gospel has been spread, love shared, and work done.

I know this to be true because I, too, am a product of the efforts of female servants.

While the debate over female leadership continues, countless women are simply, quietly serving the Lord. They are doing the work of the church, and few care what title they bear. Most of them are uninterested in the theological debates. They simply see the need and know that God has given them the grace and skill to get the job done.

Today's local officers are just like the deacons in the early church. They are concerned with spreading the gospel of Christ through practical ministries of love and service. In Christ they have found liberty—liberty from sin and liberty to serve. We remember Phoebe, deacon in the church at Cenchrea, and friend of the apostle Paul.

Phoebe (circa A.D. 55)

The worship service is over, and forty-two Christian women and men file out of the house where they have been crammed together for an hour and a half. There is lively chatter among them as they discuss the newly arrived letter from Paul, which Phoebe read. Some are humming the melodies of the songs they have shared while others joyfully surround a new convert.

Phoebe, a deacon of this congregation, discusses with several people an issue of doctrine that emanates from Paul's letter. Once free from that group, she stops at another cluster of people who are making plans for charity work. Her final stop is with the couple who will host the next worship service in their home. Finally, her work is done.

"The apostle Paul is a dear friend of mine," says Phoebe, a dignified, wealthy woman. "So many people read his writings and see him as a woman-hater. But we are friends, good friends."

Living in the city of Cenchrea, Phoebe first heard the gospel message through the clear, exciting preaching of Paul.

Cenchrea is a typical port city. Impacted by international influences, it displays a variety of cultures that seem to make everything acceptable and tolerable. Merchants are characterized by greed, and every material possession imaginable is available. There are always sailors on shore leave looking for company. The city is alive with every kind of activity, day and night.

"It is amazing that you can live in a metropolitan area and have everything the world has to offer and still feel such an emptiness inside. Jesus Christ finally filled the void in my life."

Phoebe joined the small church established by the evangelistic work of Paul. After too short a stay, Paul needed to move on to another city. These new Christians were left on their own to continue spreading the good news of Jesus Christ.

"We loved Paul and were very attached to him both emotionally and spiritually, but God wanted him to preach the good news to a new city. We wondered whether our little congregation could survive on its own, but Paul knew that God was with us. Not only would we survive, but we would grow in spirit and in numbers. We just needed to become organized."

Before leaving, Paul commissioned many of them as deacons with the responsibility of carrying out the ministry of the church.

"I was privileged to be made a servant of the kingdom of God by becoming a deacon of my church. My service here is as diverse as the needs of the people and situations I confront. In a given day, I might pray with a sick person, teach a Bible study, take food to a hungry family, secure a meeting place for worship, or meet with merchants and city fathers to discuss who we Christians are and how we can positively impact Cenchrea. I am busy with the work of the Lord, and I love it."

How did Phoebe experience such a high level of involvement in the church when Paul seemed to restrict the women in Corinth and Ephesus?

"You have to understand the world to which Paul is preaching," explains Phoebe. "In Corinth, there is the huge temple of Aphrodite, goddess of love and fertility. Worship there is incredible. Thousands of prostitutes lead people in loud, lewd behavior and mass orgies. Animal-like shrieking and public nudity are normal activities in the temple. This boisterous, frenzied religion with women at the center is also practiced by Cenchreans, and it is common throughout Greece."

To create a contrast and to show a new way, Paul called Christian women to grace and dignity. The beauty of their quiet spirit would draw others, women and men, to the Lord Jesus. And it worked. Corinth became the first Christian church in Greece.

Phoebe continues, "You also have to understand Paul's ministry style. His life motto is, 'Do whatever it takes.' Look at Paul's letter to Timothy. The congregation in Ephesus is made up primarily of formerly orthodox Jews. Timothy works with legalistic people locked into a patriarchal system that restricts women. Paul knows Christ gave women freedom to follow and serve—he said so in his letter to Galatia—but these traditional people in Ephesus are slow to change. Timothy will make better progress with the gospel if he functions from their sphere of familiarity—their comfort zone, so to speak."

The restrictions on women had been culturally induced, but Christ brought freedom. Freedom from sin. Freedom from cultural boundaries. Freedom from racial and gender biases. "This is a lot to deal with. It is a tremendous change, and at times more than people can deal with," explains Phoebe.

Unfortunately, many Christians remained bound to culture rather than enjoying their freedom in Christ. "Yes, and Paul was saying that it is the responsibility of a Christian to meet people where they are and relate to them. Once you come to understand who they are and how they think, you can better introduce them to Christ because you can speak to them in a way they will understand. The necessary changes of how you view the world will come in God's time by his Spirit."

Being a woman of wealth and noble position in Cenchrea gave Phoebe a particular advantage, because money is power. But she says, "My leadership is not about money. It is a matter of doing what needs to be done. Who, how, and when are determined by the situation of the moment. It is true, however, that having financial resources and the skills to manage them puts me into situations others can't handle. I believe Paul understood this potential and intentionally placed me in a position of leadership."

Phoebe viewed her material possessions as gifts from God. What came from God belonged to God and was to be freely shared with the people of God.

"Cenchrea can be a cruel city. There are the haves and the have-nots. Many of our converts find themselves in the grip of financial hardships because of their new standards of honesty. I'm glad I have enough to share. Some of our happiest converts are from the lowest, most abused segments of society. Their hopeless despair has turned to joy in Jesus. It is the responsibility of the Christian community to help them start fresh. I'm glad to help."

Financial help was not only given locally, but Phoebe became a patron of Paul.

"We just hit it off, you know—two strong personalities!" Phoebe winked. "Paul has the gift of evangelism and a calling to the whole world. God called Paul to this special work, and my role is to help support him. There are those called to go into all the world, and those called to support them so they *can* go. I'm the latter."

Phoebe felt her greatest honor came when Paul asked her to carry a letter personally from him to the Christians in Rome.

"Traveling to Rome was quite an honor and adventure. Women were not frequent travelers, so I was quite an attraction!" The glamour quickly wore off in dusty, bumpy days of laborious travel. "The one respite during the trip was the crossing of the Adriatic Sea. It was a beautiful, warm day with a gentle breeze that ended all too quickly at a port in southern Italy. Then several more dusty, bumpy days to Rome."

Carrying Paul's letter of deep theology and practical helps for Christian living, Phoebe was greeted with surprise and reserve. "They were shocked to see a female courier. After a quick reading, they welcomed me warmly, as Paul asked them to. The truth is, I not only carried the letter, but I was able to explain its truths and challenges because of my leadership at Cenchrea and my friendship with Paul."

The apostle himself gave Phoebe the title of deacon. Was this a special dispensation of leadership, unique to this woman?

"Remember, Paul is a pragmatic man. He has a job to do—tell the world about Jesus—and he employs any means possible to do that," said Phoebe. "He has often said he would become whatever he needed to become, or do whatever he needed to do, to win someone for the kingdom of God."

Likewise, he would use whomever he needed to advance the cause of Christ. It wasn't a debate concerning liberty or limitation. It was about getting the job done. Even Paul encountered those who wanted to spend time discussing who and how. While they discussed, other people were busy doing the work of the kingdom—a lot of them female. We remember them with gladness and see that the female laity is still a vital force today. I now speak in memory of them.

Paraphrase of Romans 16

The apostle Paul has been called the great silencer of women and the great liberator of women. Paul was one of the most influential people in the first century church.

Through his ministry, Christianity spread throughout the Western world. He is credited with many converts. He enlisted the service of many people. He set the Christian church in motion, always empowering people to take responsibility for its life, growth, and ministry. Many of these people were women. These people rise in the heavens as the cloud of witnesses referred to in the letter to the Hebrews.

In his letter to Christians in Rome, delivered by Phoebe, Paul named twenty-nine people to whom he felt the cause of Christ was indebted. Ten of these were women.

Throughout my travels and experiences in writing this book, I have met many female deacons. They are soldiers in The Salvation Army who are serving faithfully as local officers. On a daily basis they bring the message of Jesus Christ to a lost world, ministering the grace of God through their personality and programs. The church, The Salvation Army, would be something altogether different without them.

There isn't space to tell each story. But in tribute to all, this present-day cloud of witnesses, I present a paraphrased version of Romans 16:

Personal Greetings

1. Greetings to all the saints in the name of our Lord Jesus Christ who not only saved us from sin but entrusted to us his good news.
2. I thank God for each of you and all you do to fulfill the mission of the church.
3. Special greetings to Norma Baker of Rockford, Illinois. She has been a faithful servant for over thirty years, serving in almost every leadership position in

the corps. She is remembered particularly as the Young People's Sergeant Major, Recruiting Sergeant, and Corps Sergeant Major. Her strength of leadership and commitment to The Salvation Army has kept the Rockford Temple Corps strong and vital through changing times.

4. I commend our sister Barbara Newbould of Seattle, Washington, to you. While raising four children as a single parent and supporting the family by a professional career, she always found time to give of herself at the Seattle Temple Corps. Not only did she attend faithfully, but she served with distinction as the corps secretary. Her home, a place of warmth and joy, enabled many visitors to relax in her gift of hospitality.

5. Frances Dart is a tried and true veteran of the Pasadena Tabernacle Corps in California. Believing that the message of Christ's love could be presented through drama, she formed the Samaritan Players, who toured extensively in the 1950s. Her own acting skills always landed her the comedic role in the Gowans & Larsson musicals. For twenty-five years, Frances faithfully taught an adult Sunday school class specializing in the Old Testament.

6. Bandmaster Peggy Thomas is a tireless worker in Norridge, Illinois. God's gift of music is shared worldwide when she plays her cornet in concert. Each Sunday, though, finds her at the corps, where she continues to use her musical skills. Under Peggy's leadership, the Norridge Corps has developed creative ways to incorporate brass music into contemporary worship styles.

7. New Bedford, Massachusetts, has benefited for more than sixty years from the continuous efforts of Edith Levesque. She has had an effective ministry with children through her leadership in the Sunday school, the Singing Company, and Junior Band. At eighty years of age, she can still be found playing her trombone at the corps or selling the *War Cry* in town.

8. What a worker Clara Paige of Norfolk, Virginia, turned out to be! As assistant superintendent of the Norfolk School District, she used her teaching and leadership skills to build the largest Sunday school in the United States. More than one thousand children and adults attended every week. For this she was admitted to the Order of the Founder. Clara was not alone in this great effort. Her "right arm" was another female saint, Dorothy Ange. Since Clara's death, Dorothy has continued her ministry to children, preparing, at last count, 447 for enrollment as Junior soldiers and training 108 young people as Honor Junior soldiers.

9. Outstanding among women local officers is Corps Sergeant Major Dempsey Jones. Not only is she committed to her personal family but to the greater family of African-Americans who are ministered to by the Chicago Midway Corps. Complementary to her leadership skills, her spiritual vitality is a positive force for the kingdom of God.

10. Jenny Bartholomew, now in heaven with the Lord, undoubtedly received a heroine's welcome. She lived in Newburgh, New York, and had an outstanding ministry to young people. Whatever her weekday job, Jenny spent her lunch hour with a child or teenager who

attended her corps. Her diligence in visitation and her gift of encouragement transformed many lives.

11. Another leader committed to children is Orva Tompsett of Long Beach, California. By taking the Sunbeam and Guard program into the public schools, she developed more than thirty troops. Orva was a model of Christian virtue and leadership. Her life exemplified the godly character traits she so diligently taught to hundreds of young women.

12. Missionaries around the world send their love to Beverly Mercill Herival, who lives in Ferndale, Michigan, but has a worldwide ministry. Beverly maintains correspondence with all Central Territory missionaries. She has often used her vacation to visit those to whom she writes and always welcomes them into her home when they are on homeland furlough. Beverly publishes a booklet about her "overseas flock" so that others will become involved in their support and encouragement.

13. My heart is grieved for lack of space to mention the names of countless faithful lay women who found liberty in Jesus Christ—liberty from sin and liberty to serve.

14. God has blessed The Salvation Army with many talented, skilled, committed female deacons, and they have in turn blessed his church and increased the population of heaven.

15. Women and men, minister as unto the Lord. Value each other. Support one another through the power of prayer. As grateful as I am for all these industrious women, it is to God we give the glory. Amen.

CHAPTER FOUR

MYSTICS

Full of God

"I believe that religion is all or nothing. God is either first or he is nowhere with us individually. The very essence and core of religion is 'God first,' and allegiance and obedience to him first."

—*Catherine Booth*

Devotion to God calls them into deep, intense meditative communion with their Heavenly Father. An unquenchable love for Jesus persistently moves them into depths of prayer, where it is common to see visions of the love and work of their Savior. A spiritual sensitivity attuned to the Holy Spirit often causes them to hear God speaking. What seems inaudible to others is a clear, distinguishable voice to them. These are people desiring the fullness of God. These are women and men full of God. These are the mystics.

The mystic movement, which arose within the second-century church, was fully defined and practiced by the

53

Middle Ages. This had both a positive and negative impact on the place of women in the church. On one hand, it gave women a recognized and respected place to participate in the mission and ministry of the church, as nuns, through the ministry of convents. On the other hand, while women celebrated this, it was really a diminished role from what had been experienced in the first century church. Regardless of one's viewpoint, women were present and influential in the medieval church through mysticism.

Mystics have often been misunderstood and misrepresented. They are often thought of as impractical and ethereal. It is assumed their heads are "in the clouds," making them so "heavenly minded they are no earthly good." Their spiritual journey can seem so isolated and consuming that they contribute little to the kingdom of God.

Mysticism played a vital role in the Middle Ages. At a time when the church was caught up in moral corruption and political intrigue, the mystics, standing firm in the righteousness of God, fanned the flickering holy flames. The value of mysticism to the church and the kingdom of God, while questioned by some, has been widely acknowledged as a unique and important contribution.

Come now to twelfth-century Germany, and meet one of the most famous and influential female mystics.

Hildegard von Bingen (1098–1179)

Rain falls softly on the gray walls of the Benedictine convent that sits on the banks of the Rhine River. The abbey, built of stone, is sparsely furnished. There is beauty in this simplicity, but there is also a sense of cold austerity that harmonizes with the dreary conditions outside. Intimidated by the surroundings, one wonders what to expect of the Abbess Hildegard.

She is heard before she is seen. Her original chants, with their vaulting melodies, ring through the arched ceiling of the cathedral and spill outside, filling the abbey grounds with spiritual warmth. When the Mass is complete, Hildegard emerges wearing the traditional nun's habit, which covers her from head to toe. Only her face is exposed, and it seems to glow from her communion with God during the past hour. The intensity of her spirit is immediately felt: She has been in the presence of God, sharing love and devotion.

"I became abbess when I was thirty-eight years old," explains this tall, imposing woman. Although physically intimidating, her manner is kind and her spirit is warm. "My parents gave me to this convent as a tithe to God. I was the tenth child of a noble family here in the Rhineland."

From an early age, Hildegard was exceptionally bright. A voracious reader, she had an uncommon gift with words. Unfortunately, she was plagued with frequent and severe illnesses. When sick, she often saw things invisible to others, things some would attribute to high fevers. Hildegard knew it was more than that, because even future events became clear pictures in her mind. She kept all this in her heart.

"I didn't share these early visions with anyone. I was afraid of them. I was afraid of their meaning and consequences. I was afraid what people would think of me, so I kept them to myself."

When Abbess Jutta of St. Disibrod died, Hildegard was unanimously elected as her successor. Her strong spirit and leadership qualities were already well known in the abbey. Medieval abbesses headed a group of women living the monastic life and following the rule of Saint Benedict. The nuns lived a life of chastity, poverty, service, and worship. They enjoyed few comforts and always had much hard physical labor to maintain the abbey. A deep sense of isolation often permeated the sisters, but not so for the abbesses. Powerful and respected women, they sat in parliaments, attended church councils, and oversaw the affairs of clergy and lay people in their area. They were women busy with the practical, political, and religious matters of life.

Hildegard, a powerful woman by her position, was also powerful in her mysticism, her ascetic side fully developed and revered. She was committed to prayer and communion with Almighty God, and everything she did emanated from her intense spiritual life.

"When I was forty-two years old, I had a tremendous vision," Hildegard explains with moistened eyes and uplifted hands. "A burning light from heaven poured into my mind and heart, into my very being. It was the fullness of God. At that moment I was given understanding of all the books of the Old and New Testaments."

She wrote down her insights from this vision. "I shared these with my friend and fellow mystic, Bernard of Clairvaux, who forwarded them to Pope Eugenius III. The Holy Father read them to an assembly of bishops and cardinals, who endorsed my vision and my writings." These writings were bound together and became a book entitled *Know the Ways*.

From that time on, Hildegard accepted her visions and revelations as coming from God. As she committed herself to intense and regular times of communion with God, her insights into situations and people increased.

"Words of understanding flowed out of me as never before. God used me as his channel to impart knowledge and speak to people. My responsibility was to make myself available through prayer and fasting."

During the next twenty-five years, Hildegard wrote two more volumes of visions, *The Book of Life's Merits*, a handbook discussing sins and virtues, and *The Book of Divine Works*, exploring the mysteries of creation. Her visions, insights, and knowledge encompassed more than the spiritual life. Hildegard also produced two scientific studies on nature and medicine and a play, Europe's first opera.

"God is not just the Creator; he is very creative. My writings are only a small reflection of our great and glorious God!"

Hildegard, like all mystics, had a supreme source of revelation. "Everything I do is directed by my Divine Light. As I pray, the Light instructs me in what to write or who to write. I have even been told to travel and preach."

Hildegard traveled throughout Germany four times, preaching to the clergy and laity about their sin and corruption. She had had a vision of hell and felt that if the church—and many people in it—didn't repent, they would spend eternity in this tortuous place of snakes, vipers, and fire.

"I also wrote more than one hundred letters of admonition to people at every level of society . . . politicians, popes, businessmen, priests, and emperors. If God revealed to me their folly, I confronted them. If God gave me insight into their future, I told them. It was God's message. I was simply the messenger."

Not everyone received and appreciated Hildegard's revelations. She had her critics—enough critics that at one point the church excommunicated her for a short period of time.

Probably the most loved aspect of Hildegard's mysticism is her poetry. "I wrote seventy-seven poems and composed music for them to be used in the liturgy of my convent."

Written in Latin, the language of her visions, they express a love of God that makes the spirit soar. Hildegard broke the rules of the music of her day by using vaulting melodies. Sung as chants, the freedom of her melodic line reverberated through the heights of the Gothic cathedral.

"My songs are a bold musical statement that thrills some and disturbs others. God came boldly to me, and the music is a reflection of his revelation. The music that sings in me is the voice of God. Even now, when I hear the words, I can see God. When I hear the music, I can feel his Spirit. My songs are the breath of God."

Mysticism of the Middle Ages is not lost in the twentieth century. There are female mystics today. They no longer have to live in cloistered convents, and few take vows of chastity and poverty. Still, the church is filled with women devoted to God, who maintain a vital communion with the Almighty through prayer. These women with charismatic personalities and creative abilities continue to focus on Jesus and believe that he will use them to speak and minister to people in and out of the church.

Just as people were warmed by Hildegard's ascetic qualities, there are women today whose spirit exhibits the same flaming Spirit of God.

Lieutenant Colonel Virginia Talmadge
Standing before a classroom of cadets at the College for Officer Training, she held out her hand, fingers rolled up

into a closed fist. Christian education instructor Virginia Talmadge asked, "What do I hold in my hand?"

It looked like nothing. If it was something, it was extremely small. Completely stumped by the question, the room sat in silence. Suddenly, Virginia uncurled her fingers and flung up her arms, declaring, "Fairy dust!" It is a modern-day mystic's way of saying that every day holds something special from God. You don't know what it will be or when it will appear; you just have to be ready. You need to live expectantly. Expect life to be full of God!

The fullness of God first came to Virginia when she was in her early teens. Living in a small farming community in Pennsylvania, she was intrigued by a notice saying that a lady from New York City would be at The Salvation Army.

"I didn't know anything about The Salvation Army, not even where the building was located. I only knew I would love to meet a woman from New York City."

Virginia met the lady and discovered she was there to explain a weekly scouting program for girls sponsored by The Salvation Army called Guards. Not only did Virginia join the Guard troop, but she found herself at a Sunday worship service at The Salvation Army. Here she heard the good news of Jesus Christ and about his coming to earth to be the Savior of the world. That same Sunday, Virginia knelt at an altar and experienced the fullness of God for the first time.

Life was exciting in the years that followed. "I had already decided I was going to be a teacher. I used to play school with my dolls."

Plans were made to attend college, to become a teacher, to find a mate and have a large family. During this time she faithfully attended The Salvation Army corps and was fully involved in many activities. "I loved life! I loved drama, ideas, and adventure. My life was full, but over time it had become full of Virginia."

One summer evening at a camp, while she sat around the fire with her friends, God spoke, changing the direction of Virginia's life. As the program ended, while she gazed at the jumping flames, someone read this Scripture verse:

> The spirit of the Sovereign Lord is on me, because the Lord has anointed me to preach good news to the poor. (Isaiah 61:1)

Virginia can't remember the rest of the devotional. Everyone left the campfire circle and she sat alone, watching the embers slowly diminish. Out of the stillness came the realization God wanted her to be a Salvation Army officer. "I didn't want to be an officer. I argued with God. I told him I could be a good Christian teacher."

But Virginia finally realized the Scripture reading was God's tap on her shoulder, saying, "I need you; I have plans for you." At that moment, God again filled her spirit with his fullness. She knew life would continue to be full of exciting adventures because it would be full of God and full of his plans.

At twenty years of age, Virginia entered the College for Officer Training in New York City. There she met Charles Talmadge, who would later become her husband. Both Virginia and Charles are petite people—after that, their similarities seem to end. He is a businessman, good with facts and figures. She is an ascetic with a free, creative spirit. How do such different people live and minister together?

"My husband and I have always worked well together. We never compete with each other; we never hinder each other. Neither of us has ever tried to take over in the relationship. Plus, I have always seen myself as an officer. Yes, I am a wife and mother, but I am an officer, so I have always tried to do what I could according to the Holy Spirit's direction."

Officership has taken Virginia many places and directions. "I have never felt that The Salvation Army gave me an appointment. I have always felt the Army gave me an opportunity."

As corps officer at the Times Square Corps in New York City, Virginia saw God use her artistic skills. The building, located just off Broadway, had a huge picture window that thousands of people walked by each day.

"Being surrounded by Broadway, you needed to do artistic things. You needed to fit in and do something that people in that area and of that mind-set could relate to." Each week she decorated the window with items, creating a still life sculpture that depicted some aspect of God. Her goal was to capture the attention of pedestrians and cause them to think about God, even if only for a moment.

This was the birth of her self-styled *worship centers.*

Virginia spent many years of officership on the staff at the College for Officer Training in New York and Atlanta. In these appointments God gave Virginia the desire of her heart—to teach. "I loved those years. I loved every minute of it."

Teaching cadets the art and science of Christian education was her forte. By her own creative teaching style, she challenged them to present the wonder and beauty of God's Word in ways that would seize the hearts and minds of children and adults.

Her creativity impacted a teenage boy who tells of that memorable moment.

"A group of people were going on a tour of Israel. Someone couldn't go, and even though I was only a teenager, I got the vacated slot. Lieutenant Colonel and Mrs. Talmadge were the tour guides. One day we came to the Sea of Galilee. Mrs. Talmadge stood at the shoreline. She took a light blue scarf and draped it around her head as a women from biblical times might. From memory and with dramatic interpretation, she recited the entire Sermon on the Mount. The words of Jesus through her were so real that from that day on I have read and cherished my Bible." (That young man is an officer today.)

At the College for Officer Training, Virginia's dramatic skills, learned at Lake Forest College, were incorporated into worship services. There were great days in New York City in the 1950s when she teamed up with Bandmaster Erik Leidzen, creating moving presentations at The Salvation Army's "Friday Evening at the Temple" worship service. Leidzen would compose a musical arrangement for the brass band, and Virginia would create a dramatic performance using choreography and the spoken word. "I loved interpretive dancing the first time I saw it. I wanted to use it somehow in presenting Christ to the world. I didn't know of anybody else at the time doing choreography to hymns, but it seemed a perfect match to me."

Virginia also created dramas such as *Go to Golgotha*, *Decision Please*, and *Gratefully Yours*. These productions, performed and produced by cadets, touched the hearts of the Friday Evening at the Temple audiences.

Was there resistance to this less-than-traditional form of worship? Absolutely!

Some cadets, the performing artists in these gala presentations, were embarrassed to be on stage, while others thought more orthodox approaches should be used to tell the gospel message. "Also, I got word back from a leader that we in The Salvation Army didn't dance. We couldn't use dance in a public meeting."

Virginia met this resistance with her own creative energy and conviction. She reminded the performers of the greatness and creativity of God, which needed to be matched by human creativity and greatness. To Salvation Army leaders she pleaded, "Some people can hear the voice of God; others need to see it."

Because the whole world is dying for need of a Savior, and because the dying people are vastly individual in their personality, every effort and every style must be used to give out the good news of Jesus. "You see, I would just explain what I was trying to do and help them understand the art as well as my intentions. The resistance seemed to break down when people understood what would really happen and saw that it was going to be an inspiration."

Where does all this creativity come from? Where does she muster the strength to meet resistance with optimism? It comes from what Virginia calls "the precincts of prayer."

As a young officer and wife, Virginia developed an intense prayer life with her Heavenly Father. An ache in her heart always produced one persistent prayer. "We all desire certain things, and we think that this is what we need. I had been raised in a large family—eight children. I always wanted to have a big family of my own." For years she prayed that her arms would be full of children and the rooms of their home would be filled with their noises.

God didn't grant this heart's desire. Instead of many children, the Talmadges have loved one daughter, Charlene. God opened the doors of adoption, and the gift of life was given to this couple. "While Charlene did not develop, mature, or grow *under* my heart, she truly did grow, develop, and mature *in* my heart."

God's thoughtfulness showed not only in bringing a child to their home but in giving her similar gifts. Charlene, like Virginia, is artistic! The illustrations in the two books written by Virginia, *Dear God: ...Little Prayers to a Big God* and *Exploring Worship*, were drawn by Charlene. Charlene also created many of the visual aids Virginia used in her teaching and dramatic productions.

Through the years the "precincts of prayer" developed a routine and form that not only produced a deep personal relationship with God but became the fountain of inspiration for all of Virginia's creative ideas in teaching and worship experiences. The ancient mystics meditated in great cathedrals or private prayer cells, but for Virginia . . .

"I go to the bathroom!"

The bathroom is a solitary place. It is the first place we go when we wake up and crawl out of bed. Virginia begins her day in this little, quiet room. "I take care of brushing my teeth and all those little things. Then I kneel beside the bathtub and say, 'Good morning, God!' I don't want to talk to anyone else before I talk to God. I don't know how this started or why. I only know I have been going into my 'retreat' first thing in the morning for years."

In the afternoon, Virginia spends a greater amount of time in prayer with the purpose of interceding on behalf of people and bringing the issues of her own life to God. She maintains a prayer list, using it to fulfill the promises of prayer made to people, to track the movement of God in her own life, and to watch the faithfulness of God through his answers.

Praying like this takes discipline. "I am a great believer in discipline—not the 'dos and don'ts' but rather exercising control over self and living. I don't think discipline is sitting on the lid of self and holding it down. I'm disciplined because I have purposely set a pattern for my life, and with joy and self expression I have followed it."

God comes in fullness and speaks words of inspiration and guidance to Virginia during these two times of prayer. "Have you ever thought how pleasant is the voice of God? It is to be compared with the refreshing sound of running water in a pebbly brook—musical, delightfully gently, humble."

While Virginia meditates and feasts on his Spirit and Word, God commences the creative process in her. It is here that worship centers are visualized, choral readings find their form, and dramatic presentations are born. Private time with God produces a public expression of worship that benefits many.

Creative people sometimes have trouble with the routine, mundane issues of life. Not Virginia. "I never think of anything as mundane. I enjoy cooking. I enjoy scrubbing. I enjoy washing. I love life. I love every part of it!" Excited and almost bouncing off her chair, she recites:

Life, life, life!
I like his will . . .
There's so much to find and be,
Live it happy, seek and save.
Every instant is a gay adventure,
Every passing day a world to explore.

A life filled with God allows Virginia to respond by see-ing the fullness of God everywhere, especially in nature. The voice of God seems particularly clear in the world he created.

Thank you, Lord, for delicate moments of wonder and beauty. It is surprisingly easy to hear music in waves, songs in whispering winds, and laughter in rippling brooks.

It may be a flaming sunset or a bursting dawn that holds the voice of God. I may stand on tiptoe to peek into the hedge holding new life just emerging through tiny blue shells. Beauty is everywhere, it seems. Or is it just me?

If I searched, I'm sure I could find rocky paths; thorns, not roses; weeds, not grass; but I'm so happy I saw beauty and you. I wanted to join with the birds and trees, the land and the sky, in praise to God.

I just had to stand still—you were so close—I felt you breathing in all your creation. Yes, you were breath-ing in me. It was a delicate wonder.

O God, keep me always so sensitive to the beauty that surrounds me. May I always retain a glad respon-siveness to loveliness wherever I find it. May I always take spontaneous delight in the delicate, familiar bless-ing.

"The heavens declare the glory of God" (Psalm 19:1).[1]

Unfortunately, mysticism has often been misunderstood. Two female mystics, separated by centuries, have shown that their piety was neither too private nor too ethereal to

---

[1] Excerpt from *Dear God: Little Prayers to a Big God. The Salvation Army* © 1981

be of real, earthly value. Both women functioned in a public arena and offered their gifts for the good of others. For both, however, mysticism was a lifelong calling. Their ministry was effective and beautiful because it flowed from the inner sanctuary of a soul saturated with God.

Virginia has the last word. "To be what we are, and to become what we are capable of becoming, is the only end in life. Life to me is not success—achievement, getting ahead, getting to the top. The most glorious, exciting, satisfying concept of life that I know is experiencing the fullness of God."

CHAPTER FIVE

FAMILY

The Virtuous Woman

"There was added to all this the responsibility and anxiety which are inevitable in the bearing and bringing up of a family of eight children. We see indeed that her public work made an enormous demand upon her consecration, upon her devotion to the interests of souls, and upon her faith in God . . . and we her children have again and again borne testimony to the splendid influence of her life upon us, to the wonderful care for our well-being which she manifested, and we also bear testimony that she answered every call which could be made upon a godly mother."

—*Bramwell Booth*

The back door swings open, a child darts through quickly, grabbing an apple and hollering at someone outside. The hurried child approaches her mother, who sits at a table filled with bills, bank statements, and a far-too-meager checkbook. A basket of laundry and a stack of Bible

69

commentaries and Bibles lie to the side on the floor. A kettle brews on the stove, filling the room with a delicious aroma.

There is always something happening and something to do in the preacher's home! The daily life of home and family is as much a part of the pastor's world as preaching and teaching. Family life, with its many rewards and challenges, was not always encouraged for the clergy.

Medieval Christianity developed and promoted the ideal of celibacy. The church of the Middle Ages taught that God preferred a celibate life and that marriage was beneficial only for the purpose of procreation and as a remedy for lust. To truly be in God's will and a part of his special elect, women and men took vows of chastity and poverty, living their lives in cloistered monasteries.

With the Protestant Reformation, Martin Luther, a Catholic priest, not only challenged the religious traditions and dogma of the church, but he openly attacked many of its social practices, specifically those involving marriage and family.

Following his official protest in 1517, when he nailed his *Ninety-Five Theses* on the door of the cathedral in Wittenberg, Germany, Luther's ideas and writings began penetrating monasteries and convents. The protest grew in numbers, strength, and energy as nuns and priests left the cloistered life and joined the Reform movement. One of these "heretics" was Katherine von Bora.

Concealed in herring barrels, she made a daring escape from the Cistercian Convent of Nimbschem with eleven other nuns. Smelling badly, these women were delivered to Martin Luther to become his responsibility and problem. Since it was a capital offense to "kidnap" nuns, Luther had to act carefully and quickly on their behalf. All but Katherine von Bora, who rejected the arrangements made for her, returned to their homes or were married to ex-priests. An independent, strong-willed, feisty redhead, she refused Luther's options until he himself made the offer of marriage. Their marriage, family, and home life instituted the first Protestant parsonage.

For a thousand years the single, celibate life had been upheld as a Christian ideal. By their own actions of marriage and child rearing, the Reformers elevated and restored family life to the prominent place it had held previously in history. This was not just Martin's doing. His wife Katherine was a major force in the development of the modern Christian family and Protestant parsonage. To remember this unique, pace-setting woman, we go back in time to the former Augustinian monastery in Germany that was the home of the Luther family.

Katherine von Bora (1499–1550)

"As the daughter of a poor aristocratic family in Saxony, it seemed quite natural for me to be given as a gift to the church to serve in the Cistercian Convent of Nimbschem," explained Katherine von Bora. "It was a foreboding place. Friendships were not allowed, even among the sisters. Silence was enforced and we walked slowly, always with our head bowed. It was a holy place but not necessarily a happy one."

With a quick grin spreading across her round face, she continued, "One day, I'll never know how, the writings of a monk named Martin Luther were smuggled into the convent. His writings were frightening and wonderful. Without even knowing him, I feared for his life. Heretics had no future in the church!

"Over many months we received his pamphlets calling for reform. He attacked the Pope. He attacked long-held traditions of the church. He pleaded for changes, changes based on the truths of Scripture. It warmed our hearts and excited us greatly. Twelve of us took a great risk by discussing these issues and finally decided we must make our escape and join the Reform movement."

Leonhard Koppe, the father of one of the nuns, was a delivery man to the convent. He made regular visits, often with large barrels of herring. Together they devised a plan. A very large order of herring, twelve barrels, would be delivered to the convent. Once the herring was eaten and the barrels empty, the way of escape was secure. Koppe would retrieve his barrels and take them out of the convent, knowing they would each contain one nun. They would then be delivered to the residence of Martin Luther.

"The twelve of us were as much a sight as we were a smell! It was not a pleasant ride out of the convent, but the future it gave me was worth every bump, bruise, and disgusting odor."

The problem of runaway nuns and priests was not new to Luther. His Reform movement had caused many to flee to new lives. This was not to be taken lightly, as he was involved in activities that were acting directly against church policy. Each person must be dealt with quickly and carefully.

"My sisters were soon headed to their new destinies. Some returned home, and for the others Martin arranged marriages with former priests." Looking down at her simple gold wedding band, Katherine explained her fate. "A husband had been found for me, but I wanted no part of him! I became a frustration to Martin because I did not want to marry just anyone. I chose instead to reside with friends who were also Reformers. I wanted to marry Martin, but he would not consider it because he felt that being a heretic meant he would be killed soon. For two years we met privately and developed a relationship until finally he offered to be my husband. I accepted immediately! We were married quietly and quickly."

With Martin and Katherine's marriage, the Protestant parsonage was born. They moved into a former Augustinian monastery where Katy, as Martin called her, became head of the household.

"We did not live a monastic life in this place! We thoroughly enjoyed the blessings of married life. Within a few months I was pregnant, and our lives were filled with the business of a home."

The Luthers would love six children, although two of them died very young. Raising children and dealing with the realities of life, they began to develop a new model of the Christian family.

"I ran our home, which included all the business of our household. First, the old cloister had to be remodeled. I took great care in supervising this so it would become a place of solace, care, learning, and hiding, not only for our children, but for all those involved in the Reformation. It was not unusual for thirty students and guests to be living with our family."

Food supplies and meal planning also fell to Katy. "I planted fields of vegetables; I cared for an orchard; I harvested a fish pond; I raised and slaughtered livestock, brewed beer, and concocted our own herbal medicines. I was a match for the virtuous woman in Proverbs 31!"

Their six children were their joy. "You know, it was said that offspring of former nuns and priests were likely to be demon-possessed, two-headed monsters, of which one could possibly be the Antichrist," Katherine said with a twinkle in her eye. "Instead we had wonderful, lovely, spirited children who taught us as much about God as we taught them about God."

Luther believed that the family was a God-ordained institution. Basing his views upon biblical teachings, he also believed the family was meant to be the primary school for spiritual formation.

"We had a regular time for family worship. Martin loved music and would lead the children in singing. We had a time of Bible study together that was always spiced with much dialogue and debate. Every child was encouraged to participate. I believe this, along with our daily activities of caring for and sheltering people, discussing theology, solving problems, challenging church traditions—all of this done in front of our children—was their education not only for life but in the deep things of God."

The trials of life were met with a strong faith, and the tragedies with hearts of compassion. Katherine explained, "In 1527, a terrible plague struck Wittenberg. Healthy people fled the city, but not us. We felt it was our Christian duty to stay and minister to the needs of the sick, dying, and grieving. Our children were frightened, but we entrusted ourselves and them to the Almighty. He heard our prayers, and none of us were infected.

"Our children were never shielded from the struggles of a pastor's life. Martin was often discouraged by the lack of faith or weakness of faith in his parishioners. In one of these times of depression, he locked himself in his room and refused to come out. Finally, I took the door off the hinges and told him to come out and believe in the grace and power of God! Together we could bring these things to God and watch him work them out." Probably the children stood wide-eyed, watching their mother at work!

When people remember the Protestant Reformation, they primarily think of Martin Luther. They should also remember Katherine von Bora, his wife and partner! Through the force of her faith in God, her energy for life and ministry, and her commitment to her family, she has greatly impacted the Christian home. As we remember Martin's beloved Katy, we realize that many women have followed in her footsteps. We look now to one such woman, wife, mother, and keeper of a parsonage, known in The Salvation Army as the officer's quarters.

Brigadier Eva Bawden

Sitting in a comfortable chair, her hands folded on her lap, Eva smiled through the soft wrinkles on her face and began, "I'm seventy-nine years old, and my life motto is: 'Do your giving while you're living, then you'll be knowin' where it's goin'.'"

Eva Bawden and John, her husband of forty-eight years, were not inventors of the preacher's home, but their home certainly is the epitome of one. As officers in The Salvation Army, they raised five children who have each found their destiny as officers. To the five were born twelve grandchildren, some of whom are officers, and all of whom love the Lord. The family continues to grow with the sporadic arrival of great-grandchildren.

For Eva, solid family life and a fruitful ministry are rooted in her marriage. "A good marriage is primary to me. In that marriage you feel that you have a partner whom you can talk to and walk beside while finding your own sphere of influence and ministry."

She and John had only a few hard-and-fast rules to nurture their marriage. "We never went to bed angry. Even if I didn't feel responsible for the problem, I would remind myself that we shouldn't go to sleep until this was settled. Sometimes you get the silent treatment, when you know there's something wrong, but you don't know what. Always I would be willing to ask what was happening or to say I was sorry."

A second rule was to find time for themselves. "With five children around, you've got to have some time for yourselves. There were things we needed to talk out between ourselves, but also we just needed time alone. Sunday afternoons were sometimes free, and we would lock our bedroom door, taking the time to rest and talk and be together."

Money was always in short supply, but careful budgeting kept the family supplied with necessities. As each child became a teenager, he or she found a part-time job after school, learning the disciplines of work and stewardship.

Stewardship in all of life was a major motif in the Bawden home. Concerning money, Eva says, "It's the Lord's money. If I have spare money, I can't waste it, so I help others. We've helped individuals, our children and grandchildren, even other corps that needed help." Daughter Linda remembers a house rule: "Pay the Lord, pay your bills, pay yourself."

In return for this spirit of giving, Eva has experienced the constant care and provision of God in every area of her life.

But stewardship is not just about money. It's also allowing God to use you in ministry. "When I saw officers who were hurting, I would take them under my wing, listen to them, and care about their hurts. I never wanted to preach every other week, but I was happy cooking meals for various groups and doing work in the corps office. I enjoyed being with the ladies of the Home League and women in the community through service clubs like Soroptomist and Pilots Club. It's about finding your sphere of influence." Stewardship is also about knowing who you are, knowing what God has called you to do, and knowing what he has *gifted* you for.

Eva was the oldest of seven girls born to Salvation Army officers. At a young age she accepted Christ as her Savior, and at age seventeen she entered the College for Officer Training. Being the youngest cadet did not deter Eva from her calling, nor the faithful execution of ministry through her personality and abilities. Soon after her commissioning and ordination as a Salvation Army officer, she married session-mate John Bawden, and together they served forty-three years as corps officers.

Since their five children became officers, it is often assumed that there were pressures put upon the children to follow in their parents' footsteps. The children give an unqualified "No!" They testify to a house filled with love, where everyone felt important and necessary, and each was allowed to be an individual. Eva says, "If you have a dream about what you'd like to be, and pray for God's will, a door will open. Then you take it."

Each child's decision to become an officer surprised Eva. "Each child had his or her own dreams, and I supported them. One wanted to be a teacher; one wanted to be a photographer; maybe one of them talked about being an officer." Lessons in stewardship taught them that everyone should be and do exactly what God intended. Joy would come in following God's will.

"I do think that our home contributed to their callings to officership. We frequently had guests at our dinner table. As Christians we would talk joyfully about our service in The Salvation Army and the needs we constantly saw around us. We lived in faraway communities, but the world came to our home through our visitors." The realities of ministry were always before the children, but their parents' struggles and stresses were dealt with privately. "We tried never to talk about people and problems in front of our children."

In conversation Eva is such an easygoing person it hardly seems possible that circumstances could ruffle her. But they did and do! Through her varied experiences and challenges, however, Eva learned valuable lessons about managing stress and living in faith. "Life is good! As to money worries, my husband John always said not to worry. God never slumbers or sleeps, so we can. If he's worrying about it, why should you?"

When the "system" seemed to hurt them by where they were appointed, Eva recited, "Man cannot put you where God cannot use you." And to the reality that ministry is often a lonely place, she says, "I made friends out of the Army, either pastors' wives or ladies in my service clubs. You have to find some friend with whom you can just relax." Even this commitment of friendship is an act of stewardship, the stewardship of herself.

Important to the Bawden family was the evening meal. Even in the midst of a busy corps schedule, school, and work obligations, they were committed to dinner as a family. "We tried to always be together for evening meals. At these times we also had devotions. We used little promise cards and then prayed. The kids say they learned to read because they wanted to participate in the family devotions by reading their card."

Eva believes that life is about balance. She has loved and cared for her family, but she has also been actively involved in the kingdom of God through serving the community. Recently, a prominent community leader said to Eva, "What you and your husband did through The Salvation Army was a gift to our community. As far as I'm concerned, you are the 'salvation' in Salvation Army." The Rotary Club of Albuquerque, New Mexico, recognized their widespread and effective ministry by naming Eva and John Bawden as Paul Harris Fellows.

Only a couple of years ago Eva took a spiritual-gifts-inventory test and discovered she had the gift of encouragement. She has been encouraging men and women, boys and girls, and her own children and grandchildren for years. Now she knows what to call it! Even in her retirement, she remains a faithful steward of her gift of encouragement.

"I write a lot of letters. We are suffering from the loss of the art of letter writing. People call on the phone, but you can't read back a phone call! I have a telephone ministry, and I take prayer requests. I am also a prayer partner for needs in the Western Territory as outlined by the territorial commander."

Family gatherings most frequently happen now as the grandchildren get married. "These are three-hankie events," laughed Eva. At a recent family reunion, while standing with one of her grandsons and looking out over a horde of people, Eva said, "You know, it takes a long time to have this many people in one family."

This was not just a statement about quantity; it was a comment about quality. A commitment to God leads to the stewardship of self. Eva Bawden has faithfully modeled a life of stewardship, a living example of the virtuous woman in Proverbs 31. She has loved and served her God through loving and serving her family, her corps, and her community.

CHAPTER SIX

MUSIC

God Gives the Song

"One morning, Monday 15 June 1846, the miracle happened. As I opened my hymn book, my eyes fell upon the words:

> My God, I am thine; what a comfort divine,
> What a blessing to know that my Jesus is mine!

I no longer hoped that I was saved; I was certain of it."
—*Catherine Booth*

Wherever you find Christians, you find them singing! So much more than the ambiance for worship services, singing is an act of personal participation by each worshiper. And whether accompanied by a pipe organ in a great cathedral or a single guitar in a home, the simple act of singing brings the soul into contact with God.

Martin Luther, the Protestant reformer, was very aware of the power of music in worship. Believing music to be God's second greatest gift to humanity (the first being Jesus Christ), Luther made singing a central part of the Protestant worship service by calling the congregation to join in song, something quite unusual for that time. By 1523, he had written twenty-three songs and published them in what became the first Lutheran hymnal.

The priesthood of all believers was the banner of the Reformation, and music was one of the means by which all could exercise their priestly ministry. It didn't take long for a wide variety of people to become involved in writing hymns and developing different forms of music in worship.

By the eighteenth century hymnody was in full bloom. Sometimes referred to as the "Golden Age of Hymns," this era of the church produced thousands of hymns from the pens of Isaac Watts, Charles Wesley, William Cowper, and Anne Steele.

Anne Steele is one of the few woman hymnists and one of the most prolific. Drawing from her treasury of three volumes of poetry, this fragile, modest, godly woman penned the words of 144 hymns. She stands as the first female of prominence in hymnals. As a Baptist, she holds the distinction of being the first writer of English Baptist hymns. Her preeminence in church history is neither the result of being a woman nor a Baptist, but in her extraordinary contributions to the hymnody of the church.

Come now with me to Broughton, England, an obscure village made up of one long, winding street of cottages. The thatched roof on the right is the home of the Steele family, the town's only parsonage. The year is 1770.

Anne Steele (1716–1779)

Lying in bed, fragile from a lifetime of illness, Anne Steele pulled herself up, fluffed her pillows, and began with a question, "Can you imagine a church without music?"

No, I can't! Music lifts our souls to God. It fills our hearts with praise and love and helps us whisper our prayers to heaven. Worship would seem so empty and void of personal involvement without the use of music through the singing of hymns. But how did Anne become a major contributor to this aspect of the church?

"I was born into a Baptist home. My mother's father was a Baptist preacher. My father was the head deacon, and finally pastor, of our Baptist church in Broughton. He served for thirty years, often without salary. The Bible was read constantly in our home, and ministry was the norm. At an early age I accepted Jesus as my Savior and Lord, and at the age of fourteen I took my first communion and joined my father's church."

Anne showed a love of writing in her childhood and a talent for the creative use of words. "It seems I am always writing lines of verse; some I share and some I keep to myself. Words are my friends; words are my comfort."

Looking at this gracious woman, it's hard to understand why she hadn't been made bitter by the hardships of her life. "My mother died when I was three years old. This was tragedy enough, but my childhood was also threatened by tuberculosis and a serious injury to my hip when I fell off my horse. I have been an invalid nearly all my life."

Persistent illness and physical pain might be more than most people could cope with, but Anne was to experience an even greater tragedy. "God brought a wonderful man into my life, a man who shared my love for ministry while understanding my physical limitations. When I was twenty-one, we were to be married. On the day of our wedding, he went to the river to bathe. He somehow got caught in a current and was swept away. On my wedding day I stood beside my fiancé, not at a church altar but on a riverbank where his lifeless body lay."

It was a tragedy from which she would never fully recover; but that tragedy, added to the other struggles of life, filled her words with emotions that touched the deepest part of the heart. "I learned the truth of Scripture that when I am weak, he is strong. As God ministered to me, I could minister to others through words."

These stirring words were wed to suitable melodies and have been sung by people around the world.

Her sickroom was infused with the Holy Spirit's inspiration. Her words flowed from a sense of the continual presence of God: "I understood in grief there is a Comforter; in illness there is a Great Physician; in sin there is a Savior; in the darkness there is a Light; and in death we find Life."

What to write came easily because of her relationship with Jesus and her voracious reading of the Bible. Did *how* to write come as easily for her?

"I have always loved words, and they flow from my soul. I believe God has made me gifted in this area, so I am only being faithful to what he created me to be. Other than under divine inspiration, you must write simply, with imagination and a sense of wonder, surrounding it all with passion. Usually I use the common meter with four line stanzas—that's for simplicity. I believe my simplicity of style allowed so many of my poems to be translated into hymns. My words have been easily and wondrously wed to melodies that lift the soul to God. I have many friends to thank for this incredible transformation of my poetry."

Anne's family and friends were very familiar with her prolific and inspired writings, but they remained private until 1760, when a friend had two volumes of her poetry published. The book was entitled *Poems on Subjects Chiefly Devotional by Theodosia.*

"For quite some time I never attached my given name to my poems. The volumes of poetry were printed under a pseudonym, Theodosia, and my hymns were attributed to 'Steele.' No one knew that I was a woman, and a Sir Richard Steele got credit he never sought!"

This anonymity was based in her humility, but it was also a sign of the times in which she lived. Eighteenth-century society separated women and men. A woman's sphere was her home. If she were unmarried, she privately performed compassionate works of sacrificial service. Men functioned in the public sphere, and the burgeoning area of hymnody was a public expression and, therefore, not a place for women.

"It has never been about recognition anyway. What God puts in my heart flows out through my pen. As the Psalmist said, 'He put a new song in my heart.' Also, because I am so fragile in health, my ministry to the church is through words. These anonymous gifts are freely given for God to use. And he does use them!

"I remember a worship service I was able to attend. The congregation started singing a hymn written by 'Steele.' I sat quietly to listen to its effect. It was an unbelievable moment for me. At first, the congregation sang using a simple unison melody line. Then they added harmony, and to that four parts. It seemed that even six or eight harmonies were sung at one time. Every voice blended, and they breathed together. It was a magical moment when we were praying together through the song, and it was clear that we were one with the Lord and each other. It was a profound moment spiritually for everyone there, but more so individually for me. It fueled my gift and allowed me to continuously give."

Anne died at the age of sixty-three. She was still living in Broughton. On her deathbed, she whispered, "I know that my Redeemer lives!"

The second half of the eighteenth century saw an unprecedented sequence of published hymnals, most of them containing words by Anne Steele. In this era new tunes were created, existing tunes were adapted, and the use of folk and classical tunes were incorporated into the ever-developing wealth of sacred verse. New technologies developed for printing music, which allowed for a new trade in sheet music.

Music has always drawn people to the church and to God. Protestants believe in preaching the gospel, but the use of song has been almost equally effective in touching the hearts of seekers. The movement that flowered in the eighteenth century continues to evolve and expand, increasing the effectiveness of ministry in the church. Congregational singing is now one of the many avenues of the ministry of music in worship. Orchestras, brass bands, jazz bands, and rock groups all make their contribution. Choirs, barbershop quartets, trios, and soloists add their harmonies. All styles of music can be used, and everyone has the opportunity to enjoy being part of the priesthood of all believers through song.

At those moments of spiritual tenderness, moved by inspired music, which of us has not wished for a thousand tongues to sing our great Redeemer's praise! A woman in our world today uses music and her mighty voice to sing praise to God and lift souls to heaven.

Jude Gotrich

Judith, her given name, means "praise." To give praise to the God she loves dearly is her greatest desire. "A large part of what we are going to do in eternity is praise," she says, "and I want to be well practiced!" Jude's most effective tool for praising God is her powerful, yet sensitive, voice. She has been privileged to travel around the world, singing for and about the One she loves.

It might be enough to sing her praises to God, but she also prays that through her music listeners will be drawn into the wonderful presence of Almighty God. "I want to create a sound loud enough, a sound big enough, and an energy forceful enough for us to give no other response but to give shouts of praise."

This she does. One Salvationist reporter said of her singing, "Jude communicates to every part of the building with every fiber of her being."

Her intensity of worship is not the result of a haphazard approach to the choosing of music or its public presentation; it requires preparation. Jude received vocal training at the New England Conservatory of Music in Boston, but that training is not the focus of her preparation just before singing. Studying 2 Chronicles 5, which is the dedication of Solomon's Temple in Jerusalem, led Jude to understand that purification was a prerequisite to performing acts of worship in God's house. "Scripture carefully records that the priests had to purify themselves before performing their duties. From this I learned that I must purify myself in order to perform and be used by God." Therefore, before every concert, meeting, or worship service, Jude withdraws to commune with God. From places that range from offices and closets to boiler rooms, she emerges as a prepared vessel for his use.

But, before that moment of quietness before God, she has already asked for guidance on what song she is to sing. "There's a certain peace that comes when I'm going over the titles of my songs." After making the song selections, Jude finds a way to relate to them so she can minister through them. "I don't go to a song without a picture in my head. It's either a person, an event, or a Scripture portion that has impacted me, and that's what I focus on when I sing."

This focusing fills her melody with power and emotion, and God flows through her, touching someone with his Spirit. "I don't know how, but what is in my heart and mind flies through the air until it snatches someone whose spirit is weighty," Jude explains. Through the music and the messenger, God speaks, making it common for someone to approach Jude at the end of the performance and share, "This particular song had obviously been picked just for me because God ministered his grace through it."

The initial preparation for Jude's gift of music came at the age of eleven when she experienced salvation. Jude vividly remembers the day that impacted her life forever.

"My parents were corps officers at The Salvation Army in Patterson, New Jersey. There had been a big snowstorm Saturday night, but we still had to go to church. Our family of seven and one person from the neighborhood were the only people who made it that Sunday. Still, Dad conducted the meeting from tip to toe. We all participated in the service by praying, leading a song, or singing a solo. Well, that

Sunday the Lord decided to release his Holy Spirit on me. After my father's sermon, I heard God's voice saying, 'Time to go. Time to give your heart to me.' And so I knelt at the altar on that blustery winter day and accepted Jesus as my Savior."

Many years later, God called Jude to a musical ministry. This revelation came through a horrible tragedy. After completing her education, she moved to St. Paul, Minnesota, where she participated in the St. Paul Temple Corps as the songster leader. A beautiful young couple, members of her songster brigade, were brutally murdered. Jude was asked to sing at the funeral.

"I wasn't sure I could do it. We were all so incredibly grief-stricken. We were scared. We felt completely out of control. I called in prayer support from my mom and some others and then agreed to the request.

"The people were crowded into the corps. Their shoulders were up high and their necks scrunched down. Everyone was physically in a position of grief and sorrow. But as soon as the music began, and for however long it lasted, healing was occurring. As I sang, I sensed God was using that moment as part of the healing process for these wounded, hurting people. This led to the realization that I had been healed as a child to be a source of healing to others."

When Jude was three years old, she had contracted pneumonia, which led to the inflammation of her throat and tonsils. Tonsillectomies were a standard and fairly simplistic procedure in the 1950s, and one was scheduled for Jude. The doctor had predicted the surgery would take twenty to thirty minutes. He emerged from the operating room after several hours with blood splattered on his clothes and a frightful expression on his face.

He said to Jude's parents, "Your little girl is okay . . . she's alive. In order to save her life, because she was hemorrhaging, we had to stitch parts of her throat, which in turn damaged her vocal chords."

When she left the hospital, Jude couldn't speak. The doctors warned she might be mute for the rest of her life. If she did speak, it would be with a severe impediment characterized by a muffled, high-pitched, nasal tone. Being praying people, her parents activated a prayer chain to ask for a miracle. Nothing happened immediately.

"Several months passed, and I hadn't even grunted a single word. One day, while playing at my mother's feet, all of a sudden I started singing in a crystal clear voice, 'Yes! Jesus loves me!'"

Jude believes God chose that song to announce his miracle. She continues to allow him freedom to guide her in the choice of songs at each performance, because only God knows who needs a healing touch. He performed a healing miracle on her voice so that it would become a healing vessel to others. Jude understood this as she sang at the funeral of her beloved friends.

The Christian musician who ministers powerfully can also be easily misunderstood.

The regular communion of the artistic spirit with the Spirit of God, leading to revelations of music to write and words to use, can frighten and confuse fellow Christians. Jude's deep devotion to God, which puts him first and everything else second, along with her intensity of spirit, can intimidate people. Frightened, confused, intimidated—these and other reactions to the ascetic Christian musician often means she meets with resistance. Resistance to the message. Resistance to the messenger. Resistance to her methods.

Jude has experienced resistance to her musical ministry and on occasion feels personally rejected. When her style of praise and worship is ridiculed, or if her vision of how music can be used is challenged, she reminds herself that God himself called her and healed her for this ministry. It is her responsibility to remain faithful.

"Sometimes I am the only one who believes in what I am doing, so I have to be strong and stand firm. I have a coal burning on my heart that God put there, and I must be true to it." Jude's love of Jesus is stronger than any personal rejection. What the Lord thinks of her is far more important than what others think. "I noticed in Scripture that Jesus said I will comfort you—not I will make you comfortable. And my grace will be sufficient for you."

Although some people seem to believe otherwise, artists do live in the real world. Jude is married to Bert, and they have two sons, Lars and Erik. As a wife and mother, she faces the same joys and stresses familiar to us all. There are always bills to pay, mouths to feed, errands to run, relationships to nurture, laundry to fold, floors to vacuum . . . you know—life! Even the ascetic musician devoted to God and her given ministry faces the regularities, trials, and temptations of living in this world.

Since inspiration and motivation for the musician come through feasting on the fullness of God, conversely, profound despair accompanies seasons of spiritual dryness and a silent God. During one such barren period God reminded Jude of her name and said, "Jude, praise me!" For three days she obediently praised God. The circumstances didn't change much, but her faith in God's sustaining presence did. Beyond the comfort and encouragement of the Holy Spirit at that time, God also gave Jude the gift of the words that became "Songs in the Night," the title song of her second recording.

When the sun comes up brighter than the clouds can
    barely hide,
And the sun rays come dancing through the trees,
The majesty surrounding me calms the spirit of my soul.
It's so easy to give praise on days like these.
But sometimes it's so quiet when I long to hear your
    voice.
I cling to every promise of your Word.
I hide the times of anger in hopes that time will pass,
Reminded he's in all that has occurred.

But there are songs to be sung even at night.
Tho' it may seem I've been left alone with no rescue in
    sight,
And often when the nighttime falls, the problems
    magnify.
I just can't rest enough to ease my mind.
Still the quietness before him gathers might,
And I sing my own songs in the night.

My spirit seems to dangle, spinning from a single thread
And with such lowly faith, I find it hard to see.
But says to me in Scripture that his grace extends the
    bond.
I trust to find him reaching out to me.
I've learned that faith goes far beyond those sunlit days,
And sacrificial praise comes with a price.
Sometimes he wants us just to say that he is in control

And turn to him in grateful praise when we're empty or
   full.

But now I thank him for the new songs at night.
Tho' I may seem very much alone,
His presence is so bright.
He hears my words of praise to him,
And then he fills the room.
He holds me close—my spirit he consumes,
And the quietness before him gathers might
As I sing my own songs in the night.©

There is some debate in Christian circles as to whether
or not music is on the official list of spiritual gifts. Some
say that its obviously effective ministry through the centuries deem it a gift, while others say music should be couched
within other gifts, such as exhortation. The debate is not
resolved with Jude's response. "I know God uses music to
minister to people, and I know my ministry of music was
not of my doing; in fact, I had very little to do with it."

What is known is that God gives the song. He places its
melody in our hearts and the words on our tongues. Singing is an act of worship that brings sweet communion with
our God and Savior.

© 1991 Jude Gotrich

CHAPTER SEVEN

INNER-CITY MINISTRY

Such As I Have, I Give

"I seemed to hear a voice sounding in my ears, where can you go and find such heathen as these, and where is there so great a need for your labors?"

—*William Booth*

During the Industrial Revolution of the nineteenth century, Great Britain was an empire upon which the sun literally never set. Wealth poured into England from colonies around the globe, making the rich richer and creating a new middle class.

Unfortunately, the Industrial Revolution, with its newly developed factory system, created another world in England—a world of overcrowded cities, destitution, and despair. The unprecedented movement of people from farms into the cities swelled London's population from 850,000 to five million in ninety years. The social cost of such rapid growth was paid in large measure by women and poor children.

People flocked to London to find work. The factories, stifling hot in the summer and miserably cold in the winter, were quick to hire men, women, and children. They worked sixteen-hour days, six days a week, in buildings where no thought had been given to safety or sanitation and where the noise was often deafening. At the end of a long workday, these laborers would make their way home to crowded tenements, door entrances, and back alleys. The streets teemed with people at all hours of the day and night, looking for comfort in pubs and finding solace in the company of young prostitutes. Drunkenness, crime, prostitution, unattended children, homelessness—all were the social costs of the Industrial Revolution.

This ocean of misery led to reforms from the hearts of men like William Wilberforce, Lord Shaftesbury, and William Booth. While the first two men were political activists, William Booth sought spiritual reform through social strategies. Walking the streets of London's East End, he looked upon the "submerged tenth" and proclaimed, "As Christ came to call not saints but sinners to repentance, so the new message of temporal salvation, of salvation from pinching poverty, from rags and misery, must be offered to all."

The reforms of Wilberforce and Shaftesbury came through governmental policies and laws. The reforms of William Booth were personal and came through the hands of people—often women. Evangelist Honor Burrell was a light in darkest England's East End at the height of the Industrial Revolution.

Evangelist Honor Burrell (circa 1870)

Evangelist Honor Burrell sat broad-shouldered in her dark blue dress with "Saved to Save" stitched in red across

Catherine Booth, on Pentecost Sunday, 1860, wanted "to say a word."

Envoy Shirley Lindstrom Kerestesi knows both sides of prison bars. Here she shares the good news of Jesus with an inmate.

The corps officer "team," Lieutenant Colonels Maud and Jim Sullivan.

Bible stories and Salvation Army history come alive through the dramatic sketches performed by Lieutenant Colonel Virginia Talmadge.

Brigadier Eva Bawden proudly sits surrounded by her five officer children, daughters (l to r) Linda Griffin, Jan Williams, Marilyn Gregory; sons (l to r) George and Ron.

Jude Gotrich sings to the farthest corner of the room with every fiber of her being.

Major Betty Baker dispenses food and friendship to a transvestite on the streets of New York City.

(Then) Major Alice Stiles confers with Indian officers at territorial headquarters.

Women delegates to the first Brengle Institute in 1947 stand with (then) Major Mina Russell (front row, center).

Brigadier Mina Russell stands with Commissioner John Needham, national commander, in 1982 at her final Brengle Institute. With her are the principals of the four Schools for Officer Training: Major Raymond Cooper, Lt. Colonel Gene Rice, Major Donald Arnold and Lt. Colonel Roy Olford.

a full bosom. She was every inch a soldier of Christ, and every inch a woman of compassion.

"I am what it says: saved to save," said Honor. "I married young, only fourteen on the day of my wedding. We were happy enough, living in the country, my husband working in the coal mines, and us waiting to start a family."

Things went along routinely for several months, when suddenly Honor's world changed. "I couldn't imagine how my life would change when the men stood at my door to tell me Will had died, crushed to death in a collapsed mine shaft. But it changed for horror and then for good."

Having no means of supporting herself in the country, Honor moved to London to find work in a factory. Finding work was easy; living the daily grind was another thing.

"I worked twelve hours a day, unless we had to work extra hours to complete an order—this with no extra pay. The factory was built quickly, with no thought of lavatories or water. Men, women, and children by the hundreds worked side by side in crowded, hot, stuffy, unbearably noisy rooms. If someone made a mistake, they were fired on the spot. If a child talked, even to ask a question, he was beaten. On my first day of work, I watched a woman become a cripple when her petticoat caught in the gears, pulling her into the machine and mangling her leg."

Living conditions were no solace. "When I arrived in London and located work in the East End, Whitechapel Road, I was shocked to discover how difficult it was to find a place to live. I was homeless for almost two weeks. After work I roamed the streets asking people where to find a room. Most ignored me; some laughed. I slept under stairwells, in the park, and a few nights I walked all night, going into pubs for an occasional drink and rest."

Honor finally met another young woman like herself who shared a flat with two other women. She was invited to live with them, sharing an inflated rent. "It was a filthy, rat-infested tenement, but it was a place to lay my head at night."

As a shudder ran through her body, Honor continued, "It was a horrible existence. Desperately poor. Unhappy in my work. Frightened on the streets. I was given the name Honor by my parents, who taught me to live worthy of it. We were a proud people, and we held our heads high. But what a state I was in!"

Women had few options. To get beyond the point of pinching poverty, a woman could sell herself. "Hungry, lonely, and depressed, I set out one night to find a man, several men, to dishonor myself through prostitution for no reason other than money. I was going to the favorite neighborhood pub, the place other girls had found success, The Blind Beggar Saloon."

As Honor approached, she heard music, then voices. A group of men and women outside The Blind Beggar were singing songs about Jesus. "Most people gave a quick listen and left laughing. I joined the laughing crowd inside. As I made my way from man to man, I could hear an occasional word from outside. A woman's voice caught my ear."

The Salvation Army woman was giving her testimony. She had moved to London hoping to find a satisfying life. Instead she found a life of despair and loneliness. "Her words gripped my heart. I knew what she was saying and how she felt. I was lonely and despairing!"

With tears streaming down Honor's cheeks, she continued, "This lady said the solution was Jesus. I had never given much time to religion, but she wasn't talking religion. This woman glowed with happiness. The spirit in her, like a magnet, drew me. I walked out of the pub and stood in front of her. She wrapped her arms around me, and we wept. After hearing my story, she insisted I go home with her."

In the Army lassies' home, Honor was fed, bathed, given a new dress, and introduced to her Savior, Jesus. "I felt I needed so many material things, but she just kept saying, 'Silver and gold have I none, but such as I have, I give.' And what she gave me was to change my life. I got Jesus!"

Honor never returned to factory work. She immediately enlisted in The Salvation Army and was given the title *evangelist*, as was the designation of many of the women. She shared a room with another evangelist in the rescue home, "and I began my work of midnight patrol.

"Every night, as people ended their shift at the factory, I began my patrol," explained Honor. "Having spent many months in the factory and living in the tenement, I knew the underworld of Whitechapel Road. I was particularly concerned for the children and the girls who were selling themselves in dishonor."

Nightly, Honor walked the streets slowly and fearlessly. "My only purpose was to be a friend. When I arrived in London, I needed a friend. Now I could offer friendship."

Children came to know her by name, and Honor stopped to speak to each girl out walking the street in search of a man. "They've got to get used to seeing you. It comes slowly. If they get used to seeing you and find out they can trust you, they'll come when they are ready."

Prostitution is demeaning to everyone involved. "One's conscience is dulled in time. But occasionally, from a bad experience or roughing up from her pimp, a girl will come seeking help." God provided funds for The Salvation Army to open a rescue home for prostitutes in Whitechapel in 1884.

"I like to rescue the children before they get to selling themselves," said Honor. "When I'm out on midnight patrol, I'm looking for the tashers and mud larks."

Tashers and *mud larks* are the unemployed children. Tashers live with the rats in the sewers; mud larks are scavengers, eating from garbage bins.

"I try to have bits of food with me on patrol. Free food is the only way to get close to these children. Some have even come to trust me. How happy I was when The Salvation Army opened a daycare program, which included a meal, for these poor waifs."

Seven years after joining The Salvation Army, Honor was found dead in a back alley in London's East End. It is assumed she was beaten to death by a pimp. As Honor faithfully reached out to the young prostitutes, more and more looked to the Army for rescue. The midnight patrol and saving grace of Jesus were hurting business along Whitechapel Road.

Honor, who had herself experienced personal salvation through Jesus Christ, eagerly shared this redeeming work with her "flock." More often salvation was social—a piece of bread, a night of rest in a safe place, a loving hug. If success is measured by numbers of changed lives, Honor wasn't successful. If success is measured by compassionate love to the "least of these . . . the giving of cold water in the name of Jesus," then Evangelist Burrell brought much honor to the kingdom of God. She lived true to her name.

A century later in New York City, a city with conditions similar to London's East End, another midnight patrol and another Salvation Army lass carried on their work.

Major Betty Baker

Major Betty Baker and her dog, Wendy, move through the streets of Manhattan between the hours of 10:00 P.M. and 4:00 A.M., into areas known as Harlem, the Bowery, Times Square, and Hell's Kitchen. Drag queens, pushers, pimps, prostitutes, and the homeless surround them.

"These are my people! I believe that I have come to the kingdom for such a time as this."

Betty's midnight patrol ministry is a small candle of hope and love piercing the great darkness of inner-city evils. She doesn't do much or give much, but she gives what she has and what she can. "And I can always give a listening ear, a hug . . . I think that for some of them I am the only part of God that can really touch them. To know that I am part of God's plan for their lives is great."

The tools of her ministry are simple—a Salvation Army mobile canteen, a driver, her dog, and whatever food supplies are available. The van drives along the streets and "when we see the girls, we pull over."

When the van stops, the lights go on inside. The serving window slams open, and out come the cups of cocoa or soup.

"How ya' doing, Ma? Watcha' got tonight?" question the girls.

Betty explains, "I'm the mother these kids never had. Some of them have no one else to talk to." Besides a caring, listening ear, all she has is something cool to drink in the summer and something warm to drink in the winter. Usually there are cookies or doughnuts too, depending on donations.

"When I first started, I must have seemed quite naive. I remember opening up the van one night and saying, 'Hi!

My name is Betty Baker. I'm here from The Salvation Army, and this is our canteen. If you want a cold drink, just come over and we'll serve you.'

"This heavily made-up, scantily dressed prostitute looked at me and said, 'Do you know who I am?'

"No," I said.

She replied, "Do you know what I am? I'm a whore!"

And I said, "'When I look at you, I see someone made in the image of the God I love and serve.' It broke the ice, and the girls started to trust me."

Betty's faith in God enables her to see beyond the exterior—a prostitute, a drag queen, a drug user—to the people God longs for them to be. "I tell them God doesn't always love what we do, but He loves who we are. At every chance I remind them that God don't make no junk."

Her candle in the darkness works. One street person confirmed the power of her ministry: "I really believe in God. I believe in God because I see him in you," he said.

Betty was born in Glasgow, Scotland. During World War II, she met an American soldier. They were married, and Betty came to live in the United States. An abusive husband, he deserted Betty when she was admitted to a hospital while battling an illness. The only people she knew were her in-laws, who took her in. With no education or training to sustain herself, she felt very afraid.

While living with her estranged husband's family, she attended church and discovered Jesus as Lord and Savior. Betty then spent three years in Bible school, traveled to the Kentucky hills to do church work, and ultimately landed in New York City, where she met The Salvation Army.

"I worked in the library and was looking for a church. I found The Salvation Army Manhattan Citadel near Harlem, and I remembered the Army band on the streets of Scotland. I attended their church service and became instantly involved in their prison work."

Betty Baker, almost forty years old, entered the College for Officer Training in 1965. Upon her commissioning and ordination, she was appointed to corps work, ultimately ending up back in the first corps she discovered in Manhattan!

A new ministry began for Betty in July 1984. This ministry included a new culture and a new language. The ministry was a midnight patrol through the "belly of the beast," as these areas are known. The ministry began through the broken heart of the Divisional Commander of Metropolitan New York. The colonel's son, when only fourteen years old, ran away from home to New York City. His parents never knew where he was, only that he was lost in drugs and prostitution on the streets. Since The Salvation Army always helped people, why not help the night people of the streets?

With no guidelines or strategy plans, Betty was given a mobile canteen and challenged to go to the streets; not with silver and gold, but with what she had—the love of Jesus.

God has blessed Betty's service, and she delights in telling the joyful stories: "Roxanne was born Robert. At the time of her sex-change surgery, she was in good health. But she became involved with crack and rapidly began to deteriorate. She lost seventy-five pounds and began to lose control of her bodily functions. I took Roxanne to the doctor, who discovered she was a diabetic needing immediate medical help. She was admitted to the hospital where she regained her health and strength. I urged Roxanne to return to her home in Cleveland, but it wasn't until she was badly beaten and had another serious bout with diabetes that she returned home." Betty says Roxanne periodically returns to the city, still off crack and looking well. One of the success stories!

But all is not success on the streets. "Life is cheap," Betty explains. "Brutal murders are committed for a pair of sneakers, a gold chain, a leather coat, or as little as two dollars."

Her shoulders drooped as she spoke of Eve. "Eve's habitat was the Bowery, a rough area. She prostituted herself to keep up with her needed supply of drugs. We talked many times about God's love and his power to help us become what we ought to be.

"One night Eve came to the canteen, and I told her I wouldn't be out over the weekend, as I'd be away. She said, 'Okay, Major. I'll see you when you get back.'

"As she walked away I had an urge to call her back. I hugged her and kissed her on the cheek and said, 'Eve, I love you, but I want you to remember above all that God loves you more than I do.'

"She kissed me on the cheek and said, 'I love you, too, Major, and I'll remember what you said.'

"When I got back from the weekend, one of the girls told me that Eve had been murdered. We held each other and cried. I couldn't understand how God could allow this. I had spent two years trying to help this girl. I was angry. I couldn't pray. I couldn't do anything. I intended to ask for a new assignment."

Later, in her home, God came with healing peace through a favorite song. Betty sang with her accordion the words by Will Brand:

When from sin's dark hold thy love had won me

And its wounds thy tender hands had healed. . . .
By the love that never ceased to hold me,
By the blood which thou didst shed for me,
While thy presence and thy power enfold me,
I renew my covenant with thee.

Equally sad are the young children living in the welfare
hotels. "Many of them are born to crack-addicted mothers,
so their lives are already troubled by their own addiction,
AIDS, mental retardation, hostile behavior, or physical dis-
abilities. One morning about 2:00 A.M., we were serving
food at a welfare hotel. I saw a little boy walking down the
block; both of his parents were crackheads. The child had
been born with missing fingers and toes as a result of his
mother's drug addiction. As he walked toward the canteen,
he looked like he'd been physically abused. I prayed to God
to have mercy on him, and I remembered Jesus' words, 'Suffer the little children to come to me. . . .' A few days later, I
heard the boy had died. His father had beaten him unmer-
cifully for defecating in his diaper, then his mother placed
him in a tub of water that was 138 degrees. The screams of
the boy brought the police, but by the time they got there
the child was dead."

The Major and "The Man" (police) do not always agree.
Once a policeman spoke to Betty about her flock. "These
people won't change."

Betty replied, "You got that right, but I know Someone
who can change them!"

Standing only five foot, four inches, Betty seems a likely
victim but is, in fact, fearless. Friends will admit to Betty's
occasional fear of the streets, but Betty doesn't! "You can
die only once! Let's face it, a coward dies a thousand times."

More seriously, Betty adds, "I'm not afraid because I go out in the name of the Lord, and I believe the Lord is my protector."

Once a homeless man struck her, and Betty immediately returned the punch. "I hit him so hard he turned a somersault!" Fighting is not the norm for Betty, but when in the streets she sometimes has to respond like the street people. "Sometimes you have to act tough. More than once I've said, 'Man, you better be getting out of my face, or I'll punch your eyes out in the name of the Lord!'"

Fearless Betty is better known for her loving compassion and listening ear. A forty-year-old drag queen from Hell's Kitchen said, "Talking to Ma is like coming into air-conditioned comfort in an overheated situation. I look forward to seeing her every night. She's a real friend."

Three things are vital to keeping a ministry like this going: the right personnel, money, and results. Results are hard to measure on the streets. Betty defends her work. "I don't look for results. I am just faithful to the work God has given me to do. Eternity will reveal his work." The money, unfortunately, ran out when Betty retired from active officer service. After seven and a half years, the midnight patrol ended.

In her retirement, Betty goes three days a week to the Manhattan Citadel Corps to provide leadership for an AIDS drop-in center. Again, she has little to offer in the way of material goods, but, "I can make referrals for the help that is needed. I can hold their hand and pray with them. I can remind them that God loves them."

At the InterVarsity missions conference held in Urbana, Ill., a gathering of young adults exploring avenues of Christian service, Betty said, "Today's society desperately needs one-on-one contact. The strength of your youth will enable you to go forth in the name of Jesus, touching those who are hurting. We must not allow ourselves to be influenced by the spirit of affluence that is prevalent in the world today. May we, as followers of Christ, not shun any lowly service that may come our way. To give one's life to Christ for service is the greatest move we will ever make. If we choose to work for God, we must allow him to work through us, keeping in mind that duty makes us do things well, but love makes us do them beautifully."

CHAPTER EIGHT

CHURCH LEADERSHIP

Ordained as Servants

"It has sometimes been said that women preachers would be the ruin of the mission. On the contrary, it turns out that the prosperity of the work appears most precisely where the female preachers are allowed the fullest opportunity."

—*William Booth*

United Methodists granted full ordination to women in 1954. Listed as one of the "100 Most Important Events in Church History," by *Christian History* magazine, issue 28, it said that this decision was "a signal of increased leadership for women in mainline and other churches." While this is a significant milestone for the Christian church, it discounts the longstanding ordination of women in The Salvation Army and other sectarian groups. For women to have waited almost two thousand years after Jesus' inclusive ministry to be included once again in leadership through ordination is proof of the low status women hold in society, dating back to classical Greece. Jesus openly challenged this view of women.

Aristotle, whose thinking has influenced every generation, including this current one, believed that men by nature were fitter than women to command. He felt women could lead children but should teach only adults who were younger than themselves. Tertullian, a second-century church father and student of Aristotle, held an equally low view of women. He believed that Eve, a woman, was the source of original sin; therefore every woman is equally guilty of Eve's sin. Women were synonymous with sin, making them deceitful and dangerous. Tertullian didn't believe it was right for women to speak in church, nor could she claim any manly function, least of all public office. In the third century, Origen, another respected church father, said that although women should teach what is good, "men should not sit and listen to a woman."

These influences on the church of the second and third century moved women from positions of leadership in the Body of Christ to marginalized places of service and good works. In the centuries that followed Pentecost, ordination became a sacrament of the priesthood, reserved exclusively for men, as priestly functions were performed primarily in the public arena. The ancient Greek culture separated society into two arenas—private and public. Men functioned in the public sphere, a sphere considered higher than the subordinate private sphere given to women. Men were outdoor, mobile, civilized, and superior while women were indoor, stationary, natural, and inferior.

The Protestant Reformation, launched by Martin Luther in 1517, had as one of its banners the priesthood of all believers. Although women were not ordained, they were finding a public place of participation and leadership missing since the first-century church.

The inclusion of women in ministry took its greatest strides when The Salvation Army was born in 1865 (as the Christian Mission). Catherine Booth's strong convictions about the freedom of the Holy Spirit's filling and enabling, as well as her literal translation of Galatians 3:28, led to organizational mandates allowing women full freedom in ministry and leadership.

In 1870, the Christian Mission (to be later called The Salvation Army) held its first conference to design a constitution. The conference had thirty-four delegates, of which six were women. Any woman present and voting at a church conference in this era was not only unusual, it was generally considered heretical. Still, the constitution established three distinctives for the Christian Mission:

1. Power to the general superintendent (William Booth)
2. Total abstinence for leaders
3. Equality of women in ministry

Equality for women was in print but must have had difficulty becoming reality, because the 1876 conference dealt with this issue again. Frederick Booth-Tucker said of this conference, "The most revolutionary measure adopted by the conference was the appointment of women evangelists to sole charge of stations." *Evangelist* was the name given to professional personnel, and a *station* was the local unit of worship and service. In 1878, when the Christian Mission became The Salvation Army, these words would change to *officer* and *corps*. Several years later, when The Salvation Army established its own seminary, the cadet—

after successful completion of his or her training—received a commission as an officer, accompanied by full ordination in the Christian church.

During a question time in New York City on December 7, 1886, General William Booth was asked, "Why do you have women leaders?"

He replied with a smile, "Because they often lead better than men." From that came the more romanticized version: "Some of my best men are women."

One of Booth's "bests" was Annie Davis. An evangelist in the Christian Mission, she was a pioneer to a host of women officers who would be ordained and sent around the world, preaching the gospel of Jesus Christ and ministering to the needs of humankind.

Captain Annie Davis (circa 1880)

Captain Davis was the first woman appointed in sole charge of a station.

She arrived in Barking, England, in 1875, frightened but excited, without a friend but confident of the power of God to use her. God did use her! Her success validated the 1870 conference distinctive of equality of women in ministry and set the stage for the adoption of the measure in 1876, allowing women to be solely in charge.

"W. T. Stead, a journalist and friend of the Booths, once wrote William, saying he was cruel to send frail women to undertake such exhausting work," Annie said with a laugh. "William replied, 'You would never make a general. A general must not be afraid to spend his soldiers to carry a position.' I carried three positions solo before I married."

Sitting in her office, now a colonel and married, Annie wore the dark dress uniform of The Salvation Army, accented by a small, sterling silver shield at the front of her collar. She and her husband, William Ridsell, met when serving as evangelists in the Christian Mission. Later they became the first Territorial Commanders of the British Territory.

Through dark brown eyes, flashing with passion, Annie told her story. "I was a young Christian woman. Not poor, but not from a family of wealth. I was not uneducated, but I didn't have the opportunity of higher education. When I was fourteen years old, I was on my own to make it in the world. No one in my family was a Christian, but friends introduced me to Jesus as the Christ. On my own, I discovered I had a flair for adventure and a strong personal confidence within. On a Saturday I was out exploring the wonders of London. I heard fiery preaching from a man standing in front of The Blind Beggar Saloon. He was passionate. He was forceful. He was full of the love of Jesus. He was William Booth. I followed him and his group back to a meeting, and there, to my surprise, I saw a woman preaching. William led the singing and the testimonies. Catherine preached and called many to the penitent form."

Annie Davis would find this small evangelistic group every Saturday in London's East End, always following them to the indoor meeting.

"After several weeks, the Booths noticed I was always present on Saturday night. First Catherine approached me in friendship. Then William came in his boisterous, enthusiastic way, determined I was a Christian, and without asking any further questions, said, 'God needs you, and we will give you a place to serve him.' With that, it was done. I quit my job at the linen mill and began my service for God in the Christian Mission."

The years from 1867 to 1870 were years of rapid growth in the Christian Mission, and Annie was part of this exciting time. A tireless worker at the Mission, she led many sinners to the Savior. "In 1873, after a series of open-air meetings in Barking, it was determined that a station should be opened. The Barking station was opened, experiencing the typical ups and downs of Satan fighting against the wonderful miracles of God. By 1875, a change of leadership was needed, and I was sent in charge."

Without great gifts of eloquence or management, Annie set her will to do her best and trust in God. "When I arrived, I was shocked to find a debt of seventeen pounds! Mr. Booth made it very clear that each station was to support itself."

In fact, Superintendent Booth said no personal pay could be drawn until all debts were canceled. Annie continued, "I gathered the missioners and explained the serious situation. Each of them pledged a greater support, but being poor folks they couldn't give more money. Together we decided to increase our open airs, thus increasing our collections.

"The Swan with Two Necks was our regular Saturday-night stand, which gave us many souls to witness to, and they were generous souls at that! We decided to add an open air on Friday as well, meeting in front of The Pig and The Whistle. It was there God brought us George."

George was half boozed up by the time the open air began. As he tells it, Miss Annie dragged him from the pub and into their procession to the hall for a meeting. As Evangelist Davis tells it, George staggered out on his own. The ending of the story is the same, however!

"After preaching, I invited those who wanted to know the Savior to come forward to the penitent form. George came quickly, seeking mercy from Jesus. He got properly saved, giving drink and the devil the boot!"

Barking station grew numerically each week. "The reason for the growth was our visiting. Every day I would go from house to house, meeting people and getting to know them, and inviting them to our meetings. My goal was to knock on the door of every house in Barking."

Evangelist Davis never met her goal. A letter came from London, signed by William Booth, moving her on to Shoreditch, her second station.

"This was a bigger command than Barking. We held meetings three nights a week in the Apollo Music Hall. Open airs were conducted at the pubs on Friday and Saturday night. Sunday began with knee drill, followed by a meeting; the Band of Love in the afternoon; and a final meeting in the evening."

Beyond that busy schedule Annie gave oversight to a religious literature shop and a small refuge for friendless, penniless girls. "The financial demands were so great I was instructed in the use of begging letters. Begging letters were sent to the wealthy merchants and businessmen in town, asking for their support for our work. We found many who believed in us and supported us financially rather than by personal involvement."

A crisis came when the Apollo Music Hall evicted the Christian Mission. "This crisis opened new doors for us. We ended up renting an old pudding shop with a porch, like the other shops had. Each Sunday morning the neighboring merchants would stand on their porch, crying, 'Buy!

Buy!' So we stood on our porch and cried, 'Come, it's free! Come, it's free!'"

Efforts were made to stop the missioners from this unusual practice. "We simply asked the magistrate, 'If they allow the butchers to stand in their shops and on the pavement all Sabbath morning, crying, "Buy! Buy! Meat four pence, half penny a pound," why may we not stand and offer salvation cheaper still?'"

The objections of the merchants were indefensible, and many sinners found free grace in Shoreditch at the pudding shop. But Evangelist Davis' greatest joy was with the children in the Band of Love.

"Little Patty particularly caught my attention. This darling came from an awful home. Patty got sick, and I visited in her home for a fortnight, bringing milk and biscuits."

Patty died, but even still, there was victory. "At Patty's funeral service her drunken father and backslidden mother both got saved."

From this victory emerged a new idea: "Your-Own-Flesh-and-Blood Meeting." Annie explained, "The missioners gathered together to pray for our families. As each knelt, I asked them to tell God two things: one, what you have done for the salvation of those for whom you are praying; and two, what you will do for them in the future to get them saved. In the weeks that followed, Christians were being revived and sinners were getting saved!"

At the height of the revival another letter came from Superintendent William Booth. Yes, Evangelist Annie Davis moved again, this time to Poplar. It was now 1878, and the Christian Mission had ninety-one evangelists at stations, of which forty-one were women. At Poplar, Annie was given a young man as an assistant.

"It was wonderful to have a helper. It was easier to get everything done that needed doing and to keep all the meetings and services going.

"And," Annie smiled widely, "it helped me have a little time for myself."

A couple years earlier, Annie Davis had met William Ridsell at a Christian Mission conference. From that time they had corresponded and were developing a serious friendship. "William was the evangelist at Kettering, so it was difficult to be together too often, but having a young assistant made it possible for me to get away from time to time."

While their courtship continued, so did the work in Poplar and Kettering. The work of the Christian Mission also continued to grow stronger and wider in scope. In 1878, the Christian Mission became The Salvation Army. "This was a most exciting announcement. With it came a secure structure, a uniform, and I became a captain! My general was William Booth."

Every army needs a flag! Catherine Booth designed and created The Salvation Army flag—a central yellow sun on a field of red, bordered by royal blue. Catherine presented the first flag to Captain Mrs. Reynolds, officer in charge of the Coventry Corps, at a great meeting attended by five thousand people.

With excitement, Annie explained the colors. "They define our basic doctrine. The red stands for the blood of Jesus. The yellow sun symbolizes the fire of the Holy Spirit, and the blue represents a holy life that brings the promise of eternity in heaven. Our motto, 'Blood and Fire,' is emblazoned on the sun. The flag is not just a banner to follow;

it is our message to the world!" (In 1882, the sun was changed to a star.)

Poplar Corps, with Captain Davis and her young lieutenant, was going well. "I was training my lieutenant to be an officer of the 'Blood and Fire' sort. He was learning every day, but I was glad to hear in 1880 that a training home for men and women had been established. Its purpose was to teach the Bible and the business of government and the church to candidates for officership."

Not only was the Poplar Corps progressing, the courtship between Annie and William Ridsell had progressed to the point of asking General Booth's permission to be wed before 1878 ended.

"The General was not too happy with our request for marriage. He was depending on our faithfulness in our corps. When we told the General we would still be faithful, just at the same corps, he shared his frustration. He said that when people got married, he often lost his best leaders."

General Booth said there was some "strange mistake in our organization contrary to our principles" that happens at marriage. Where before there was one plus one, suddenly it is "one plus naught."

Annie Davis and William Ridsell were married. They now forged a new dimension in officership—a team ministry. Each ordained, each held responsible for the corps, each committed to ministry—a team that together became greater than its parts.

A model of the synergy and strength of team ministry in the western United States is Lieutenant Colonels Maud and Jim Sullivan. Together they have impacted the kingdom of God, touching thousands of lives and expanding Salvation Army ministry in their corps appointments.

Lieutenant Colonel Maud Sullivan

"Jim and I were both Salvationists, and met at Redwood Glen camp when we worked on a summer camp staff. I knew I was called by God to be a Salvation Army officer, so I was looking for a fella' who also wanted to be an officer. Jim caught my eye! We both had just graduated from high school, and I found out he would be attending Azusa Pacific University. I followed him there!" Maud's characteristic laughter, a breathy panting, was followed by a wink.

Married in their third year of college, Maud and Jim completed their bachelor of arts degrees, and, following graduation, entered the College for Officer Training in San Francisco. Commissioned as Salvation Army officers and ordained in Christian ministry, their first assignment was in San Diego as corps officers. Here they would begin designing their own unique team ministry.

"You have to be a team because there is so much to do, so many responsibilities. As a team you can do more; it's that simple." Maud explained that as a team, she and Jim "work together, apart." And when looking at the multiple needs of their worshiping congregation, needy people, the community, and the administration to run them all, "we slice up the pie, each taking pieces we handle well."

According to Jim, "We hold each other up. She has strengths where I have weaknesses, and I have strengths where she has weaknesses. We have different leadership styles, and we relate to people in different ways."

In 1991, the Western Territory of The Salvation Army presented the Sullivans the Frontiersman of the Year award.

Jim believes it was in recognition of their team ministry. "We received it together, and both our names are on the plaque."

Maud's pie pieces have followed the seasons of her life. "Years ago, when we started having children, my time and responsibilities were portioned differently than they are now. I believe in being a good mother and spending time with my four children, but I was also called into the ministry. It's a balancing act." Robin, one of Maud's daughters, remembers her as "a good mom and a busy mom."

Pastoral work in the corps, the church part of The Salvation Army's ministry, has been the focus of Maud's leadership. She has used her bachelor of arts and masters degree in Christian education in her ministry. As a student of the Bible, Maud is an excellent preacher and teacher, utilizing her innate creativity. From expositional sermons, chalk talks, and dramatic monologues, her consistent teaching of the Bible has brought many to Jesus and nurtured hundreds of others.

"A team ministry is hard on a marriage. You work together; you minister together; you eat together; you parent together; and then you go to bed together. That's a lot of being together!"

Maud and Jim have learned over the years that communication is the key to an effective team that still loves each other when they go home.

Since their ordination and commissioning as officers in 1960, Maud and Jim have been in corps work with the exception of three assignments. "We were stationed at the Honolulu Boys' Home for delinquents; we were on the staff of the College for Officer Training; and we were divisional youth secretaries. Then we were sent 'back' to the corps."

Said facetiously, Maud speaks passionately, "Corps work is not a demotion! It's the best place to fulfill one's calling to ministry. As a corps officer, I find freedom to be and do exactly what I feel God created me to be and do."

Soldiers of the corps see Maud as the consummate pastor. "Colonel Maud visited me before and after my surgery. She even sat with my husband during the surgery." Many soldiers report, "She prays for me; she spends time with me; and she is always there when I need her. I feel like part of her family."

While Maud shared her life story, she was folding laundry for an elderly couple in the corps. "I've been doing their weekly laundry for a couple years now. They aren't well and have a hard time getting this done. It's no problem for me, and I'm glad I can help."

Pastoral work also includes training. "Colonel Maud has taught me how to work with the children in my Sunday school class. They come from dysfunctional homes, and I don't always understand their behavior." Another explained, "She trained me to lead the women's group, the Home League. I work with the ladies, conduct the weekly meeting, and fill out the monthly report. Colonel Maud attends, but I lead."

This ability to incorporate soldiers in leadership, while strengthening the corps, has met with some resistance on the administrative level. Corps officers are directly responsible for everything that happens in their appointment, with specific responsibilities falling to the woman officer. "But you see, I'm not good at some of those things," says Jim, "So I find a woman who is, and she becomes the one responsible. Divisional headquarters doesn't always understand that they are better off relating to the woman who is skilled and interested in the program. Instead, they continue to communicate directly with me, and I . . . continue to let my leader lead!"

This seeming defiance is no defiance or "cause" to Maud. "It's just logical. The Army believes in the priesthood of all believers and in spiritual gifts, plus the Army allows women to serve in many areas. Currently I'm giving overall leadership to the corps, the worshiping congregation, as well as several social service programs in the community. I don't have time to directly lead one small program, but I do have a woman who is committed and trained."

Colonel Maud, her self-appointed title, is also seen by some as championing a feminist cause. "I gave myself the title of Major Maud when we moved to Las Vegas in 1983. My children were grown, and I entered a new season of life. I was able and willing to invest myself totally in our ministry. I took leadership over the corps, the Women's Auxiliary, the Family Service office and employees, as well as giving leadership to many aspects of the Christmas work. I was working side by side with my husband, but now I was working equally. He was known as Major and I was known as Mrs. Don't get me wrong. I love Jim, and I love bearing his name, but this isn't about our marriage. It's about my being an officer, holding my own commission and ordination. It seemed only right that The Salvation Army, which gave me a place to serve, would also recognize my commission."

Many saw Maud as the consummate feminist when her name began appearing in print without recognition of her marital status—Major Maud Sullivan. She was corrected, teased, and mocked, but she held to what she knew was true. "Galatians 3:28 says there's no difference between male

122

or female; we are all one in Christ. I thought, *When I came into the Army, that's what it was all about.* According to Catherine Booth, I have a right to the ministry God called me to. I didn't think it was different for men or women."

It isn't different now. In 1995, married women officers in the United States, who were previously addressed through their marital status, would now be addressed by their rank as their husbands always had.

Leaders of The Salvation Army recognized the Maud and Jim team, and in honor of their years of effective ministry promoted them to the rank of lieutenant colonel in 1995, a rank reserved for upper-level administrative officers. Because of its timing, the significance was almost lost to Maud and Jim. "Jim had just had a heart attack. He was lying in intensive care, recovering from bypass surgery. Besides being worried about him, I was running the corps, keeping our multitude of services going, and hosting the visit of General Eva Burrows. When Commissioner Peter Chang, the Territorial Commander, called, I thought it was my son-in-law playing a practical joke. Luckily I went along with the joke until I realized it really was the Commissioner! The Commissioner told me I was promoted to the rank of lieutenant colonel, offered his congratulations, and asked me to please tell Jim that he, too, was promoted to lieutenant colonel!"

Jim reacts, "It was an honor but not so much to us as an attempt to honor the role of corps officers."

The busy life of a corps officer is unending and certainly oblivious to rank. "Now we were colonels, but we had just lost our assistant officers, so I was doing everything again," Maud explains. "I was doing the youth work, organizing van routes, running the Sunday school . . . on top of all my other responsibilities."

Ministry is not about rank or position. Jesus said the servant should not be greater than the master, and the Master modeled a life of service.

Maud, ordained as a servant, has faithfully served for thirty-seven years. One of her soldiers said of her, "She's very dependable. She's always there—during bad times and good times. Colonel Maud reminds me of the bunny that keeps going and going."

How does Maud keep going? "We've learned you have to take some time off. Beyond vacations, we try to take Monday off. Exercise is important too. I swim often; Jim walks every day."

There is spiritual exercise as well. "Every morning, before leaving for work, I spend time reading the Bible and praying. I don't use devotional books. I read Scripture consecutively, sometimes stopping to do a little study. When I pray, I follow the ACTS formula: adoration, confession, thanksgiving, and supplication."

Maud doesn't have a life motto, but has lived her life on two passages of Scripture: the previously mentioned passage in Galatians and Philippians 4:4–7: "Rejoice in the Lord always. I will say it again: Rejoice! Do not be anxious about anything, but in everything, by prayer and petition, with thanksgiving, present your requests to God. And the peace of God will guard your hearts and your minds in Christ Jesus."

CHAPTER NINE

MISSIONS

Set No Borders to His Strength

"'Go ye into all the world,' said Jesus, 'and preach the gospel to every creature.' What is implied in this commission? Would it ever occur to you that the language meant, 'Go and build chapels and churches and invite the people to come in, and if they will not, let them alone?'

"'Go ye.' To whom? 'To every creature.' Where am I to get at them? Where they are. Seek them out; run after them wherever you can get at them and preach the gospel. If I understand it, that is the meaning and the spirit of the commission."

—*Catherine Booth*

People are everywhere. The streets are teeming with noisy life and the stink of garbage, ginger, urine, the vendors' smoky food, incense, sweat, hot curry, and diseased cows. Lavish rugs hang against a backdrop of squalor. Rainbowed saris, glass bangles, loops of silver and gold jewelry are displayed, yet a residue of extreme poverty clings to everything. The air is fiery hot and sticky humid. Dry mouths fill with dust, creating a desperate craving for water that must be boiled before drinking to prevent hepatitis or typhoid.

India, turning the corner into the twentieth century, was little different from India through almost five thousand years of history. On the surface were colorful layers of culture and custom, but under the facade was a country locked in the horrors of a fatalistic religion.

Hinduism consists of a pantheon of gods, numbering into the thousands, and these gods are represented in a thousand different ways. The gods are present everywhere, and almost every moment of the day is governed by some sort of religious ritual. A trinitarian godhead consisting of Brahma, Vishnu, and Shiva represent three objectives to their disciples—eternal life, knowledge, and joy. These are obtained through union with god at nirvana, which one moves to through reincarnation, hopefully arriving finally at a higher caste of life. Therefore, those who follow Hinduism blandly accept their place in life as a result of karma, the law of cause and effect, which determines one's birth. Dharma, the duty to keep caste, is the disciples' responsibility if they hope to be reincarnated into something better. This influential religion creates a society where community is a foreign concept; where personal aspirations, hopes, and dreams are unthinkable; and where natural talent is squelched.

This is the India that westerners confronted during the surge of the missionary movement that marked the nineteenth century. Enabled by the technology of the Industrial Revolution that opened the world for travel, and empowered by the ever-widening knowledge of millions lost in spiritual darkness, Christians began reaching out to countries and cultures ignorant of the gospel of Jesus.

The missionary movement began in Protestant churches in England and spread quickly to the United States. Societies were formed with the purpose of raising money and recruiting missionaries. This was accomplished through education, which included printed materials and public meetings with visiting missionary speakers. Responding to the inspirational pleading of men such as Hudson Taylor, founder of the China Inland Mission, hundreds of couples moved their families to foreign mission fields. The focus was on China and India, countries where, according to Hudson Taylor, "four thousand people died every hour in darkness, Saviorless and hopeless."

The mission field was hard on marriages and particularly hard on women. Expected to go with their husbands and to live in primitive conditions, even if they felt no call, missionary wives were expected to keep the home life stable and provide a refuge for their weary husbands while homeschooling their children. Also, the missionary wife was expected to learn the native language so she could help with services and ministries offered to native women and children. Some wives collapsed under the pressure and returned home, leaving their husbands to carry out their calling. Many women were exhausted into illness, often death.

But the need remained, and the call for workers continued. With the loss of many wives, and a growing reality that the customs and caste systems of the eastern cultures prohibited men from being effective to half the population, unmarried women were encouraged to respond to the call of God.

Two single women, separated in age by fifty years, over-lapped in missionary service to India. Both came to India because of a distinct calling to the foreign mission field. Both young women stepped into a culture completely foreign to their own, embracing a land of alien sights and sounds. In hot, humid, overcrowded, caste-bound India bloomed two women whose lives found their likeness in the gloriosa superba. The gloriosa superba, a lily native to southern India, seems to grow best where only God would think to plant them. They are not a tidy, pot-bound plant but a flower found in rough, rugged places.

Amy Carmichael, born in Ireland and influenced by the nineteenth-century missionary movement, responded to the cry of an inner voice, "Come over and help us." Motivated by a simple life motto: "Love through me, Love of God," Amy applied for service through the China Inland Mission. Denied for health reasons, she looked to the Keswick (holiness) Convention, who not only sponsored her but enabled her to find her life destiny—service in India.

Amy Carmichael (1867–1951)

Amy Carmichael sits under a tamarind tree strewn with flower garlands and paper lanterns. Children play games in the garden with one little girl as the center of attention. "It is Leela's Coming Day celebration. She has been with our family for three years now; today she is four."

Leela is just one of more than a hundred little girls living under the protection of the Dohnavur Fellowship, rescued from a life of temple prostitution. "It is a most horrible part of the Hindu religion. Infant girls are sold to the temple and become members of the devadasis caste, dedicated to the gods. They are condemned to live a life of immorality and vice, suffering from disease and often death, resulting from infections and venereal diseases contracted through their religious prostitution. They have no choice. They know nothing but this evil . . . unless God in his mercy intervenes through us."

Amy Carmichael came to India to share the gospel of Jesus Christ. Born in Ireland and raised in a Christian home, Amy experienced a personal relationship with Jesus at the age of thirteen, but it wasn't until she was seventeen that the values of God became her own.

"One rainy, Sunday morning in Belfast, my family was walking home from church for our midday meal. I spotted a ragged old woman struggling with her bundles and instinctively went over to help her. She didn't belong in our neighborhood, and our neighbors who walked alongside us were shocked that I would even touch the woman. Against their disapproving stares, I helped this woman along, although I was very embarrassed. I heard a voice and turned to see who was speaking to me. No one was there. It was the voice of God, saying, 'Gold, silver, precious stones, wood, hay, stubble; every man's work shall be made manifest: for the day shall declare it, because it shall be revealed by fire; and the fire shall try every man's work of what sort it is. If any man's work abide . . .' (1 Corinthians 3:12–14)."

If any man's work abide! That moment changed Amy's values. Nothing would ever matter again but the things that were eternal. She was seventeen years old when she threw herself into service for God. She held children's meetings, organized a morning watch of prayer and Bible reading, and volunteered at the YWCA, but she truly found her ministry in the slums of Belfast with the *shawlies*.

"Thousands of shawlies lived in Belfast," Amy explained. "They were girls and women who worked in factories. They were poor and could not afford coats or hats, so they bundled up in big plaid shawls. Few, if any, went to church. They certainly weren't welcome in my Presbyterian church! So God led me to them with his message of love. I visited them in their neighborhood and homes, making friends with them. I saw the poverty and crime they faced daily."

Amy convinced the minister of the Rosemary Street Presbyterian Church to let her hold a church service for the shawlies. The services grew in numbers until they outgrew the church. They needed their own hall, one that seated at least five hundred.

"This was my first experience in prayerfully trusting God to supply our needs." Rather than take up offerings in the local churches, Amy felt God should do the supplying. "Don't you think God could make his own people want to give without being asked? The Bible tells us to ask him and not to beg. It would be safer just to pray; if the money comes, we will know it was of God."

The hall was built and named The Welcome. This method of fundraising and seeking God's will became Amy's hallmark. The 170 acres occupied by the Dohnavur Fellowship in India was purchased over ten and a half years in 171 different financial transactions. Each land purchase, no matter how small, was a sign from God to advance the work as he supplied the needed money. Never once did they have property debts!

At age twenty-one, Amy sailed for England where she began a work among the shawlies of Manchester. After several years of hard work, long hours, and inadequate food, Amy physically collapsed. She was welcomed into the home of Robert Wilson, whom she called "Dear Old Man." Wilson's wife and daughter had died, and Amy's father had died. They adopted each other, caring for one another, including Amy's widowed mother and six of the children still at home.

"Robert Wilson took me to the Keswick Convention." Keswick was a series of meetings that preached the deeper Christian life called *holiness*. "I had been two years with the DOM at Broughton Grange, and we had grown as close as a father and daughter. When I heard again of the thousands dying daily without the hope of Christ, my spirit grew restless. Then I heard a voice as clear as the voice in Belfast."

"Come over and help us," was the plea to Amy.

Amy was confused. Mr. Wilson, as well as her mother and family, depended on her. Her health was fragile. "I had a lot of reasons why I could not go, but no reason I ought not go." Amy wrote her mother, saying, "He says go—I cannot stay." Her mother and the Dear Old Man gave their blessing.

With excitement, Amy applied to the China Inland Mission, but she was rejected following a doctor's examination. The Keswick Convention had formed a mission committee and chose Amy as their first missionary. She sailed for Japan on March 3, 1893. As the days passed on the ocean liner, Amy realized, "How terrible it would be to live an ordinary life—content with ordinariness—to be busy here and there and lose the thing committed to me."

But Japan was not to be her place of service. After fifteen months, Amy's health broke down again. "I was sent away to rest. Discouraged and confused, I remembered a speaker in Japan saying, 'Set no borders to his strength.' I prayed and committed myself to the will of God. He would place me where he needed me."

On November 9, 1895, at the age of twenty-nine, Amy arrived in India. She would never leave that country for a homeland furlough or speaking tour. India was Amy's destiny, and she died at Dohnavur on January 18, 1951, at the age of eighty-four.

Back under the Tamarind tree, a girl came running to Amy to show a butterfly she had caught. "Amma, look what I have!"

Amma is Tamil for "mother." With the obvious love and delight of a mother, Amy responded, "Pearleyes, isn't God good to create such wonderful things for us to enjoy? Let it live for others to enjoy too."

Pearleyes was Amy's special child. The ministry of Dohnavur developed through Pearleyes, and Amy knew the loving relationship of child and mother. "Upon my arrival in India, I was placed in the Tinnevelly District and joined with other women, some missionaries like myself, and some Indian converts. We called ourselves the Starry Cluster. We traveled from village to village in a bandy (small covered wagon drawn by oxen), meeting people and sharing the good news of Jesus. One of my companions, who became so important to me and Dohnavur, was an Indian convert named Ponnammal.

"Evangelism was our work for several years," explained Amy. "Then Pearleyes came into my life, and things began to change."

Pearleyes was five years old when she escaped from the temple. By the providence of God she found Amy and threw herself into Amy's protection and keeping. "She truly had big, round, pearl-like eyes. Each evening I would return from the Starry Cluster work, and Pearleyes would greet me with love and enthusiasm."

With tears welling in her eyes, Amy continued, "I gave Pearleyes a doll. Through that doll she told me of the horrors of the temple, and what it meant to be a servant of the gods. This little girl knew only pornographic pictures, illicit sex acts, and erotic dance movements. At age five she knew too much evil for this to be wild stories out of her imagination. I realized if this was true for my little one, it must be a story that could be repeated by hundreds of innocent children. We needed to do something!"

Doing something was God's intent! Slowly the rescue work of Dohnavur began with Amy's familiarizing herself with the secret underground traffic in children. "I stained my skin with coffee grounds, put on a sari, and realized why God never answered my prayer at three years of age to have blue eyes like my mother. With my brown eyes, stained skin, and brown hair, I moved unnoticed through the temple courts and back streets of the village."

This daring adventure taught Amy how and why children were sold to the temples. "There are a number of reasons why parents would allow such a hideous life for their daughter. First is the value of sons over daughters. If a man had only daughters, he would give one to the temple as a ritual son. Second, if a man had too many daughters, he would sell one to the temple for financial reasons. Daughters were expendable; they were easy cash for a hungry family. Finally, if a mother died and a wet nurse was needed, or if a father died and money was needed for the family, selling a daughter to the temple was not only practical but considered a meritorious thing to do."

Little girls didn't stand a chance until God brought Amy Carmichael to India to found the Dohnavur Fellowship, a haven for lost children. "It wasn't until nineteen years later that we rescued our first boy. We discovered boys were dedicated as musicians to the gods. This was a smaller problem, but one we found ourselves involved in."

The ministry of rescuing children was not without criticism. The public press and fellow missionaries were upset with Amy and wanted her driven from India. Still displaying hurt and unbelief, Amy described the criticism. "The secular press felt I was just another Brit destroying their culture and customs. They were incensed by my book, *Things as They Are*, which told of the awful realities of Indian life and worship." The book circulated around the world and was reprinted thirteen times, giving a dim view of the land and customs of India.

And what of the criticism of the Christian community? "It was worse! I was told I wasn't doing true missionary work; I was only a nursemaid. I was reminded again and again that those who preached did not do work with their hands. Changing diapers, filling milk bottles, and babysitting was not spiritual work."

When she conformed to Indian culture by wearing a sari, Amy was criticized for growing too close to the people. If she wore Western dress, she was criticized for not being culturally relevant. People were divided in their view of her, and Amy became the reason for discord and division among the churches and missionaries. Finally, although single women were specifically recruited, even her singleness became an issue. "In India no woman can live without marrying; it is their custom. But I never wanted to be married, and there were other women like me. Together with seven other nurses, we formed Sisters of the Common Life, with vows of singleness as a primary calling. We were effective for God, yet we were under fire from his people."

Amy felt that if God were not in their work, the financial support would stop. It never did. Dohnavur grew in numbers and property. Thousands of children were spared the destruction of temple life. Hundreds grew up to be Christians, many staying to carry on the work of Dohnavur.

When Amy was sixty-four years old, she was walking around a house, inspecting it for possible purchase. As she walked and prayed, she fell into a pothole, breaking a leg, dislocating an ankle, and jarring her spine. These injuries led to a series of inflammations, infections, and further injuries, which made her an invalid for the last twenty years of her life. Although nothing was as it had been, Amy continued to seek God's will. "God never wastes his children's pain." From these years of pain and suffering came thirteen books, bringing the number to more than fifty from her pen.

That day in Belfast—when Amy heard the challenge to build a life using only gold, silver, and precious stones— became a moment that changed her life forever, and the thousands of others who would be touched by her.

Another woman living later in this century also found herself in India with a ministry to young people. Her ministry, although less dramatic in the telling, is just as profound as it, too, is built on the eternal.

Brigadier Alice Stiles

Captain Alice Stiles arrived in India in 1946, five years before Amy Carmichael died. Both women lived in southern India, but they never met. Both were involved in building the lives of children, although Alice would see her ministry develop in more diverse ways.

When I met Brigadier Alice Stiles, she wore a dark blue cotton dress with matching blue cotton pants. A white drape came from her shoulders, crossing in front. Alice was wearing the Salvation Army uniform of Bangladesh. Bangladesh and not India? But that's the end of the story. Let's start at the beginning.

Alice has big brown eyes that sparkle with the joy of life. She got her dark eyes and tan skin from her Puerto Rican mother. Alice, the middle child of five, was born May 3, 1919, to Salvation Army officer parents who were stationed in Hawaii. When Alice was eight, her mother died of tuberculosis. Her father, who had changed denominations, was now pastoring a Pentecostal church in Hilo. It was a difficult time for the family. The two youngest children were taken to be cared for by a family on another island, and the two oldest children were sent to a sanitarium because they also had contracted tuberculosis. "It was just Dad and me at home, and it was during those years he thoroughly spoiled me."

When together as a family, theirs was a serious home without much laughter. "Dad was very strict, and there was no fooling around." Strictness was blended with a serious spirituality. "I was raised in a Christian home. We had prayers three times a day. Our faith was a serious thing, but I wasn't to understand it all until I was in college."

Having the desire to teach in a public school, Alice hoped to go to the University of Hawaii after high school graduation. There wasn't enough money to make this possible, so Alice took a job as the cook at The Salvation Army's Hilo Home for girls. Good news came to Alice.

"During that year my high school decided to give scholarships to the university, and I was to receive one. Between the scholarship and my earnings for the year, I was able to enroll at the university. I moved to Honolulu and lived for room and board with a doctor and his family, helping a little around the house and with the children.

"Three years into my studies, I had a crisis of faith," said Alice. It was serious enough that she removed herself from the university. "I didn't know what I believed, and I didn't feel I had any right to be a teacher if I didn't know what I believed." At this same time, the doctor's family moved to the mainland, leaving Alice without a home. She turned again to The Salvation Army. Brigadier Frances Beard, an officer who had been stationed at the Hilo Girls' Home, was now in Honolulu. Alice looked to her for help and guidance. As it turned out, the Honolulu Girls' Home (now Waioli Chapel and Tea Room) needed a cook. Alice accepted with a caveat: "I want you to understand that I don't know if I believe in God, and you must never call on me to pray in public—not even to say grace.

"I found God in the Army," Alice stated emphatically.

Weeks had passed, and Alice dutifully sat through the weekly chapel service. They were beginning to permeate her heart. One chapel they sang:

I will follow thee, my Savior,
Thou hast shed thy blood for me.
And though all this world forsake thee,
By thy grace I will follow thee.

"The leader said not to sing unless you really meant it. I started to sing and couldn't. I started and stopped two or three times. It seemed they kept singing it over and over again. Maybe some people thought it was too long, but it was God delaying the service for me because I eventually sang it with them. It wasn't a matter of going to the altar; I just sang with them."

Praying beside her bed that night, Alice confessed her sins and claimed by faith belief in God and his Word. "I knew I had to go to the altar to make it public. At the Sunday night meeting, when the altar call was given, it was just too far away. The next Sunday night I sat closer, but it was still too far. Three or four Sundays passed, and each time I was getting nearer. Eventually, I sat in the second row—finally close enough! I settled the matter with the Lord, and it included becoming a soldier of The Salvation Army and going to the College for Officer Training."

The year at the Honolulu Girls' Home provided needed mentoring. "Frances Beard influenced me by her spirituality and her ability to keep on doing things that needed doing, always with a sweet spirit. Brigadier Kay McClellan taught me to laugh. I grew up in a family where life was earnest, serious, and intense, but Kay taught me life was full of laughter. Now I probably laugh too much."

Alice left for the College for Officer Training in San Francisco months before bombs were dropped on Pearl Harbor. Fearful for her family, and sitting in blacked-out rooms thousands of miles from home, she was glad to have another friend from the Hilo Girls' Home, Captain Helena Sainsbury. Helena became a lifelong friend and prayer supporter.

Her first appointment as a lieutenant took Alice to El Paso, Texas. While working in the home for unwed mothers, Alice felt an urging for missionary service. "It wasn't a voice or the result of a speaker's words. It was just a feeling that came over me. I wrote the first of three letters stating my desire for missionary service. I didn't feel called to any country." Alice set no borders to God's strength!

"Confirmation of this feeling came through my father. He had not been pleased with my becoming a Salvation Army officer. When I told him of my desire to be a missionary, however, he reminded me of a childhood statement: 'God is wanting me to be a missionary.' Now my father understood why God had me in the Army."

Four years after her commissioning as a lieutenant, Alice boarded an ocean liner for India. Her departure was not without strain. A friendship with a young man attending the waterfront corps in San Francisco had begun. But Alice had fixed her eyes on the goal, frustrating her friend. "Alice, all you think about is being a captain. You're not prepared to give it up!" For Alice it wasn't about being a captain; it was about doing God's will, and his will was going to India.

Captain Stiles's first appointment in India was to the Catherine Booth Hospital in Nagercoil. There she would teach English to the student nurses and perform secretarial duties for the chief medical officer, the famed Colonel Dr. William Noble. Alice had little to do with his work with leprosy and eye diseases but said, "Sometimes Dr. Noble would call for me while he was operating. Once when I came into the operating room, he said, 'Oh, now Miss Alice, let's see, why did I send for you?' He couldn't remember. Since they were about to start the operation, he said I could pray for the patient.

"Upset, I said, 'You called me away from my language lesson for that?'

"'Well,' said Colonel Noble, 'come and pray for this patient in his dialect.'"

139

"Well, I couldn't do it, and he knew it!"

India is a country of villages, hundreds of thousands of them, creating thousands of dialects. Alice never mastered any one dialect and usually had to use translators, but said, "Although I never had the gift of language, I was given the gift of understanding. I understood enough to know what was said and especially to know if my students were learning correctly."

Alice was transferred to the Boys' Boarding School in Nagercoil. The Salvation Army usually provided primary school education in villages. Their ministry was almost exclusively to the "outcast" of the Hindu caste system. Following World War II, The Salvation Army expanded education to the higher grades through boarding schools. Outcast boys from the villages would come to the boarding school for further education and vocational training, giving them a chance for a better life.

Alice became "mother" to hundreds of boys! Affectionately called Major Ammal (Tamil for *woman*), Alice was principal of two boarding schools: Nagercoil and Ahmednagar. "The population was made up of boys and girls who walked in from the surrounding villages and returned home each day, boarders who were Salvation Army officer children and boarders who were orphans. It was the orphans who became my family."

The orphan boys who became her sons spent their holidays and seasonal breaks with Alice. She arranged proper marriages for them and keeps in touch with several to this day. She has a growing list of grandchildren too. Alice speaks of one son, Suresh, with typical maternal pride. "Suresh and his wife became Salvation Army officers. I was told that he is one of the best officers in the Western India Territory!" She quickly unfolded a wallet of pictures.

Alice returned to the United States twice to finish her degrees. She obtained a bachelor of arts degree in education and a master's degree in psychology.

Upon returning to India after one such trip, Alice learned she was being sent as principal to the boarding school in Ahmednagar, in the state of Maharastra. The news shocked and disappointed her. "It was a time that the boys who had grown up in the boarding school in Nagercoil were moving out. They needed someone they could turn to. I felt I was being taken out of the picture, and I was sure it could not be God's will. Also, southern India was green and beautiful, but Maharastra is dry, broken down, and decrepit. I began thinking about other things I could do with my life. I came very close to quitting.

"On the train to Ahmednagar, I was utterly miserable and felt this wasn't going to be the place God had for me. I shared my struggle with only two people, and I counted on their prayers. Almost a year had passed, when on a Monday I joined a group of young people at a cottage meeting and suddenly it dawned on me, 'This is the place the Lord wants me to be.' Just like that, peace came to my heart. It was wonderful."

While still the principal of the boarding school in Ahmednagar, Alice was also appointed as territorial youth secretary. Her love of young people made this extra responsibility a joy.

Later she was appointed as a divisional commander, serving successfully in two divisions. While divisional commander in Poona, Alice also held the position of territorial youth secretary and principal of the College for Officer

Training. As important as all these appointments were, Alice lived a simple and humble life because of the shortage of money and resources.

All three positions called for traveling from village to village. How did she get around? "I walked a lot. We had a vehicle but seldom money for petrol. Many people used bicycles, but I couldn't seem to manage riding one. For a time I had a moped, but after a spill riding over loose gravel, and getting stuck in mud on a rainy day, I returned to walking. I didn't mind; I like walking. I just had to carry my own water because the days were usually hot and dry."

Ultimately Alice had to admit, "Three appointments were too much to handle, and the territorial commander and I had a chat." Alice was given one appointment: principal at the College for Officer Training. This was not an administrative desk job. While running the college, she also taught many of the classes, helped to translate materials, wrote lessons, and supervised outings to neighboring corps for field work training. They were busy but happy days.

At sixty-five years of age, Alice retired from service in India. At her retirement service at the training college, she was given the highest compliment by an Indian colonel. "You have been a Maharastran among Maharastrans." She lived humbly, served faithfully, and was accepted and admired by the people.

Sacramento, California, became her retirement home . . . for a short time. Alice was enjoying friends and family, especially during the Christmas holidays. Returning home one evening from a Christmas party, Alice thanked the Lord for a very lovely day. "But it seemed the Lord said to me, 'It's been a lazy day, hasn't it, Alice?' And then I read in my devotional book a verse: 'This command I have for you, my brothers, from our Lord Jesus Christ himself, have nothing to do with lazy Christians.' I just wondered why the Lord was so hard on me."

These words prepared Alice for a phone call from Lt. Colonel Ray Robinson, divisional commander in Northern California. "Alice, I've just come from a meeting in which we talked about opening a corps in Fairfield, and we feel that you would be the ideal person." After a slight resistance, Alice prepared herself to move and bring The Salvation Army to an unsuspecting community.

A few years later, Alice once again retired after successfully beginning the Army's work in Fairfield. This time she moved to Medford, Oregon. Again she was living happily until one day, "I had this feeling that the Lord wanted me to go someplace, and I should be ready to go. I didn't know where it was, and I was waiting to find out. I saw people were needed for The Salvation Army's expansion into Russia. Even though I wasn't interested in the cold of Russia, I still volunteered!"

The letter making herself available for service was sitting on General Eva Burrows' desk in London, England, when an emergency need arose. The principal at the College for Officer Training in Bangladesh had become ill and was sent home. "This was the first session of cadets to be trained in Bangladesh," explained Alice.

Since Bangladesh was a Muslim country, special permission was granted to The Salvation Army for this training session. With the loss of the principal something had to be done quickly, or else this unique opportunity would be lost. General Burrows said, "Contact Alice Stiles. She'll do it."

"Immediately, I was storing things, packing other things, and getting visas in order." In February 1993, Alice was in Bangladesh trying to teach six cadets in a language she had no time to learn!

Again her gift of understanding language carried her through. During her fifteen months in Bangladesh, she celebrated her seventy-fifth birthday!

The ordination and commissioning service of the Crusaders for Christ session was held in June 1994. Alice reported with a huge smile, "At the conclusion of the commissioning service, twenty-five young people came forward declaring their desire to be Salvation Army officers." The future is bright because of God's purposes, which are executed through the lives of servants like Brigadier Alice Stiles.

"So many people say, 'Oh, you have sacrificed a lot.' I have never sacrificed anything. People preach about bearing a cross. Well, I've never borne a cross. Whatever God reveals as his will, it must be good. 'Doing the will of God . . . The best thing I know in this world below is doing the will of God.'"

CHAPTER TEN

TEACHERS

Torches to Be Lighted

"Read and study the Word, not to get a mass of knowledge in the head, but a flame of love in the heart."
—*Samuel Logan Brengle*

Through a teacher's classroom pass all members of every profession. Teachers have been both highly honored and highly criticized throughout history. Most of us can remember our best and worst teachers.

There are dull and uninspiring teachers, but there are also teachers who kindle in students a love of truth and purpose. Jesus was a teacher who *enkindled*. Following the calling of his disciples, Jesus' first act was teaching at the synagogue in Capernaum. People were amazed, not only at his skill, but by the authority with which he spoke. Throughout his earthly life, Jesus was first and foremost a teacher.

The first-century Christian church grew in numbers and knowledge through the preaching and teaching of the apostles, who had been instructed by Jesus. The gospel needed to be proclaimed and explained. In fact, Christianity without explanation would have led to failure. Truth without understanding will not last.

Paul was the greatest teacher in the first-century church. Nearly half of the New Testament is filled with his teaching, instruction, and explanation of Christianity. In Paul, we see how the gospel spread by the passing of the torch from generation to generation—from Jesus, to the apostles, and on to Paul; who then passed the light of truth to others.

In Corinth, Greece, Paul met two teachers: Priscilla and Aquila. Paul took this teaching team with him to Ephesus, leaving them there while he traveled on to Antioch. Priscilla and Aquila heard Apollos, a God-fearing Jew, teach about Jesus. He spoke with fervor and accuracy, but it was an incomplete teaching. Apollos knew Christianity only from the perspective of John the Baptist. John's gospel ended when Jesus' began. There was so much more Apollos needed to learn. So Priscilla and Aquila taught Apollos the fullness of salvation, grace, and sanctification.

Priscilla was a woman and Aquila was a man. In biblical narratives the order in which people are named is significant. In this teaching team the female teacher is named first. Teaching was considered the public arena in the ancient world, and a woman usually functioned in the private arena of home and family.

It is as significant that a woman is participating publicly as it is significant that she is named before the man, suggesting greater skill in teaching.

More significant is the freedom displayed by this female friend of Paul in light of the puzzling message to young

Timothy, where he says he would not permit a woman to teach a man. If Paul's personal opinion was meant as an eternal biblical principle, why didn't God direct Aquila to instruct Apollos, and why did the Holy Spirit inspire Luke to record this event in the Book of Acts, naming Priscilla first?

Paul's words to Timothy have caused much pain in gifted-but-marginalized female teachers. Traditionally church leaders have restricted women to teaching other women and children. This not only diminished the importance of teaching, but denied a great number of people the blessing of learning from skilled female teachers.

More recent scholarship on this puzzling passage has revealed new insights of interpretation. Rather than restricting women from teaching and holding positions of authority, it is believed Paul is dealing with arising heresies. The concern is for women to carefully learn the truth and refrain from teaching error. This interpretation would support the inclusion of women that Jesus modeled. It also reveals the wonder of Christianity that women were allowed to read, learn, and teach Scripture, in contrast to rabbinical tradition that forbade women even to touch the Torah.

This passage will continue to be debated and, while it is, women will continue to find God-ordained places to teach. Their students will be children, women, *and* men. The light of truth that has been passed on through faithful teachers from generation to generation will continue to illuminate lives, often through the teaching of women.

Two women who have used their God-given gift of teaching to influence and inspire several generations around the world are Henrietta Mears and Lieutenant Colonel Mina Russell. Both held a personal goal to teach, but neither could have guessed where teaching would take them in God's kingdom. Neither Henrietta nor Mina was restricted in teaching, nor did they seem to concern themselves with Paul's words. God opened doors of instruction for both of them.

Henrietta Mears (1890–1963)

On most Sundays in 1931, at Hollywood Presbyterian Church, more than four thousand children, women, and men filled the Sunday school classrooms. Two and a half years before, 450 attended each Sunday. This phenomenal growth contrasted with a slow and consistent decline in Christian churches throughout North America. European higher criticism (analysis of the Bible as a historical document) and modernism, a philosophy that undermined the authority of the Bible, had fueled the decline. The disillusionment resulting from World War I was followed by the Scopes trial, where biblical Creation won but modern liberalism triumphed in the introduction of the scientific ideas of evolution.

In the midst of this decline, why was one church experiencing such growth and excitement? A high school chemistry teacher from Minnesota had recently been hired as Christian education director. Henrietta Mears, sometimes referred to as a female "apostle Paul," explains, "From my childhood I have been committed to the Bible as the textbook for life."

Wearing a blue dress with butterfly sleeves, red earrings, bracelet and necklace, bright lipstick, polished nails, several rings on her fingers, and a fashionable but outlandish broad-brimmed red hat, Henrietta says emphatically, "Don't ever say I'm just a Sunday school teacher. You are a teacher in Christ's college. Be proud you teach!"

Her eyes, with a smiling glint in them, peer through thick eyeglass lenses, and she adds, "I wear my hats for my college boys, and they love them."

Henrietta Cornelia Mears was born in Fargo, North Dakota, the youngest of seven children born to Margaret and Ashley Mears. "My father owned several banks in the Dakotas. We were a family of wealth, living in high society. Maybe that's where I get my flair for fashion!"

When she was young, the family moved to Minneapolis, Minnesota. "My parents were fine Christians, and we attended the First Baptist Church where I received Christ as my personal Savior."

A precocious, intelligent child, Henrietta often surprised her parents. "When Mother would do our daily family Bible readings, she would often dumb-down the words to make them more understandable. This always upset me, and I would ask her to read as is, knowing God would help us understand."

On returning home from her first day of kindergarten, Henrietta was disgusted. "Mother, kindergarten is only to amuse children. I have been amused enough; I want to be educated."

She graduated from high school among the top of her class, going on to the University of Minnesota. In 1913, she graduated from the university and accepted a teaching position at Central High School in Minneapolis. "I spent thirteen happy years there teaching chemistry. It was there the love of students was planted in my heart."

As a senior in high school, Henrietta, along with a friend, attended a series of meetings at church. "Together we heard the call and committed our lives to full-time Christian service. We were willing to go wherever the Lord wanted us to go and do whatever he wanted us to do."

Her friend went to Japan on missionary service, but Henrietta had no clear word from God. "I wondered if something was wrong with me. Was I not worthy of missionary work? Was I not able to hear the voice of God?"

As it turned out, Henrietta's leading was to attend the University of Minnesota.

During her years of high school teaching she met the love of her life. "He was in banking, a life I was familiar with. He was a wonderful man, but not a Christian. He often said he admired my religious convictions but had no convictions of his own."

This relationship became a spiritual struggle for Henrietta because of her strong Christian beliefs and lifestyle.

"I prayed fervently, reminding the Lord that he had made me the way I was. I loved security. I loved home. I loved children, and I loved this man. What was I to do?"

Henrietta broke off the relationship, sacrificing the love of her life for the gospel. "I prayed again, 'Lord, you promised to fulfill all my needs. I trust in you alone.' And he has never failed me. Marriage was never an issue again." Some say it wasn't an issue because her true love was the apostle Paul!

In her thirteenth year of teaching, Henrietta took a year-long sabbatical, traveling the world with her sister. Margaret and Henrietta traveled throughout Europe during the summer and wintered in Southern California. "The purpose of the sabbatical was not just to travel but to assess my goals for the future. I was sensing God had new plans for me."

While in Southern California, the sisters attended Hollywood Presbyterian Church. "The pastor, Stewart MacLennan, asked me to come on staff as the Christian education director. After much prayer I knew this was God's doing."

Henrietta was an amazing combination of intellect and devotion to spirituality. She was also an administrative genius, a motivator, an encourager, and a leader. Under her direction the Sunday school grew by leaps and bounds.

"First of all," Henrietta explains, "we had to deal with the curriculum. It was horrible! If the material was biblically sound, it was unattractive, inefficient, and provided no continuity from year to year for the student to grow from. The material that was educationally sound was liberal and did not teach the Bible as the authoritative Word of God. Also, I was upset by the comments of two students. One said, 'Sunday school just got dumber and dumber.' The other said if he had to take a test on the Bible, he would flunk."

She had no option but to write the curriculum herself. "First, we divided the students into grade/age levels so they would be with other students of the same learning level. Then I began writing lessons for each grade level. My office assistant would mimeograph the lessons and add pictures to the younger students' lessons."

The goal was not to entertain the Sunday school students, but to teach them the Word of God and train them for Christian living. "Everything we offer youth must be excellent. Their association with the gospel must be of the very finest in every way because, as I tell my teachers, each student is not a bowl to fill, but a torch to be lighted."

Not only did this revolutionize Hollywood Presbyterian Church, but word got out to other churches, and requests for copies of the material began to escalate. "At first we made extra copies of each lesson and sent them to those who requested them. As the requests grew, we sent a master copy for them to make their own copies. But even that got out of hand. A more productive system had to be established."

In 1933, with the help and dedication of members of Hollywood Presbyterian Church, Gospel Light Publications was established. "We took our materials to a printer who could mass produce them. Our first warehouse was a garage, and a dining table was the office."

Today, Gospel Light Press is a leading publisher of Christian education materials. In 1961, Gospel Light expanded and formed Gospel Literature International, which adapts and translates curriculum and books, publishing them in more than one hundred languages.

Driven by a conviction that she was training the next generation of world leaders, Henrietta personally took on the college group. "Sunday school class was a time of learning. I taught them the Scriptures, although they accused me of always returning to the Book of Romans. We had hundreds of class members, so group leaders were picked. I personally discipled the group leaders."

The officers and leaders of the college group were expected to be at Henrietta's house every Saturday at 6:00 A.M. for a prayer meeting. One youth recalled, "Miss Mears taught us to be bold before God, to ask great things on God's behalf. As we prayed, always on our knees, we heard and felt her grasp the throne of God and give it a good shake."

High energy, enthusiasm, humor, excellence, and driving intensity characterized Henrietta—and she expected the same from everyone else. Wednesday night was a more casual Bible study and sharing time for the college group. One Wednesday evening Henrietta sat quietly through the sharing time. When it ended, her voice boomed out, "That has been the most ridiculous testimony time I think I have ever heard! All we have been talking about is silly little things that don't amount to a hill of beans. There hasn't been one word about winning the nations for Christ."

Henrietta formed The Fellowship of the Burning Heart, a special discipleship group. Only a few young men joined her in this group. "To be a part of this fellowship, one pledged absolute consecration to Christ," explained Henrietta. "One of the members of this fellowship was Bill Bright, who became the founder of Campus Crusade for Christ."

Committed to worldwide evangelism, Henrietta called all her young people to the same intense commitment to Christ. "I felt we needed a place of retreat where God's Spirit could work more intensely on the young people—a place where commitments could be made."

Through a series of events that only God could have directed, Forest Home Conference Center in the San Bernadino mountains was purchased. Camps and conferences were planned for young people during the summer months. "I felt youth needed to get away from their routine to experience Christ in a special way. Everything planned was spiritual in nature and purpose. Forest Home is not a place but an experience. The center of camping is Christ."

One young man who experienced Christ in a special way at Forest Home was Billy Graham. In 1948, Billy came to a conference and while there experienced a spiritual crisis. He was sincerely questioning the authority of Scripture. After private prayer, Billy met with Henrietta. "We prayed together, and God settled the issue with Billy."

Billy Graham went from Forest Home to conduct the 1949 Los Angeles evangelist crusade, which launched the worldwide ministry that continues to this day.

God used Henrietta in huge portions, but only because she willingly gave herself to every opportunity. "There is no magic in small plans. When I consider my ministry, I think of the world. Anything less than that would not be worthy of Christ, nor of his will for my life."

Henrietta died when she was seventy-three years old. She worked tirelessly for the Lord, even on the day of her death. She once said, "Enthusiasm starts a hard job. Determination works at it, but only love continues until it is finished." It was abandoned love of Jesus that carried Henrietta to the finish.

Between her impact on Christian education material, and the men and women to whom she passed the torch of truth, the sun never sets on the places influenced by this great woman. Another "torchlighter," Lieutenant Colonel Mina Russell, has also influenced the world through her teaching.

Brigadier Mina Russell

To an excited and pleased crowd of thousands, Commissioner Robert Thomson, Eastern territorial commander, called Brigadier Mina Russell to the stage of the Great Auditorium at Ocean Grove, New Jersey. The event was a congress gathering to celebrate Christ! The weekend guest was General Eva Burrows, international leader of The Salvation

Army. The occasion of this moment was the admitting of Brigadier Mina Russell to the Order of the Founder.

In 1917, on the fifth anniversary of General William Booth's death, his son Bramwell, then general, instituted the Order of the Founder. This honor was devised to acknowledge the unique and dedicated service of any officer or soldier that would likely have come to the attention of the Founder himself. When asked why she thought she got this honor, Mina humbly responded, "I suppose it's because of the Brengle Institute."

It was because of the Brengle Institute, held annually in Chicago since 1947, and because Mina took this Institute around the world in the later years of her life. In presenting Mina to General Burrows, Commissioner Thomson said, "One of the Army's foremost exponents of holiness and prayer, Colonel Russell was a member of the planning commission for the first Brengle Institute held in Chicago in 1947. Since then she has participated in Brengle Institutes and prayer seminars in all four USA territories and many other parts of the Army world, including Canada, Kenya, Zimbabwe, Nigeria, Ghana, India, Sri Lanka, Singapore, Indonesia, the Philippines, Hong Kong, Japan, and Korea."

God's plan for Mina's life would revolve around her involvement with the Brengle Institute. Mina's personal goals of education, teaching, and travel would be fulfilled, in large part, through the Brengle Institute.

Born in 1903, Mina grew up with her sister and brothers in Lawrence, Massachusetts. Her parents were Christians and actively involved in the local Salvation Army corps. As a child, Mina had a simple but true faith. When she became a teenager, however, Mina experienced a crisis of faith.

"I was confused and upset. I couldn't do anything my high school friends could do. I couldn't go to the prom because I was in The Salvation Army. I asked my father for permission to dance, and he said, 'I can't give you permission to do something I think will hurt you.' Like any other teenager, I figured my parents didn't understand. I took dance lessons from a boy at school and went to the prom anyway! It should have been a great evening. I had the dress I wanted. I was with a boy who hired a limousine, which was a lot in those days, but I had a terrible time."

Confused in what she believed or didn't believe, Mina worked at a mountain hotel after graduating from high school. "I felt restless. For six weeks at the hotel, I was part of the gang . . . but I wasn't. At the end of summer I came home, unsettled. I didn't feel I had left the Lord, but I felt chained to things I was supposed to do and not free to do what I wanted."

Mina spent time praying, seeking God's will for her life. She attended the annual youth councils, and during a prayer time the congregation sang:

> Love so amazing, so divine,
> Demands my soul, my life, my all.

"Suddenly I knew what I was to do. I was to be a Salvation Army officer. It came with such conviction, I've never forgotten that moment."

Two years passed before Mina entered the College for Officer Training. It could have been longer because she had two dreams to pursue: a college education and travel. As she worked, saving money for college, Mina evaluated her calling and her dreams, finally surrendering them to God for his greater purposes. "It might not sound like I gave up much in these two dreams, but it was huge to me. I thought if I never travel, or never go to college, this is still what I have to do."

At her commissioning and ordination Mina was appointed to the College for Officer Training. During her nine years on the college staff, Mina met a man to whom she became engaged. "I was engaged for three months, but I knew this was wrong for me. It wasn't that marriage was wrong. I felt I loved him, but it just didn't seem right. I had questions, but thought I'd just go ahead with the marriage and work things out. There was such nagging inside, I finally broke the engagement. It wasn't about him; it just wasn't right for me. I've never regretted that decision. I've never wasted time dreaming about the children and grandchildren I never had. I found my destiny in being single."

During the Great Depression, Mina was appointed to corps work. "I learned so much during those years. I received three dollars a week for salary and had holes in the bottom of my shoes like everybody else."

During these years, her desire for education was rekindled. "As I watched people, I wondered why they did what they did. I had thought everybody was naturally good, but learned they aren't. The Depression brought out a lot of bad things in people. Many lived in hovels, drank too much, and did things for fun that you had to forgive. Other people were just trying to survive and looked to The Salvation Army for what help we could give. What we had, we gave, although it often wasn't much. Mostly we became a part of their lives, which allowed us to share spiritual things."

Mina's first dream was realized when, in 1936, she was assigned to territorial headquarters in the Education Department. It was a desk job, except for summers when she administered a camp for city children. "I soon realized this was my chance to go to college. My high school credentials allowed me to get into Columbia without testing, and I borrowed money for tuition." For the next seven years, when Mina wasn't at her appointment, she was taking courses at Columbia, one and two at a time. The end result was a bachelor of science degree and a master's degree, both in psychology.

Again, Mina was appointed to the College for Officer Training, this time as the women's chief side officer. She was responsible for all female cadets, holding them accountable to the rules and regulations for deportment and dress. Many feared her as the strict and stern drill sergeant, but others knew her kind and caring spirit. A retired officer recalled, "When we were in training, children were not allowed to live with their parents in the dorm. Our daughter had to stay with relatives for nine months. When we had a day off, we didn't have enough money to visit her. Mina found this out, and once every two weeks she would put an envelope in our mailbox with enough money for us to get to New Jersey and back."

In 1947, Mina was scheduled to go to a conference, but something happened and she was denied this opportunity. She would soon learn this disappointment would lead to her greatest opportunities for God. During the time Mina would have been away at the conference, a meeting was called to plan the first Brengle Institute. Mina was assigned to represent the Eastern Territory at this meeting. This chance appointment resulted in thirty-five years of teaching and travel—a dream come true.

Commissioner Samuel Logan Brengle was a spiritual giant in the early days of The Salvation Army. He had a special ministry of preaching and teaching, promoting the doctrine of the sanctified life and the indwelling presence of the Holy Spirit. Brengle wrote nine books, all on Christian holiness. The Brengle Institute, an idea of General Albert Orsborn, encouraged officers into a deeper spiritual life. Mina explained further, "The Institute's purpose is to introduce the officer to the possibilities of a deeper life of consecration, and, for those who know this consecration, to revive and renew the Spirit's work in their life."

Each summer officers from around the United States gather for ten days of spiritual retreat in Chicago. It is an honor to be assigned to the Brengle Institute. "It wasn't always seen as an honor! The first Institute met with heavy resistance because people felt the implication was they were not good enough officers, not spiritual enough; they somehow needed to experience a spiritual renewal." The resistance quickly subsided.

Mina's particular contributions to the Brengle Institute were her sessions on prayer. Mina believes that "a deeper life in the Spirit is developed, maintained, and enlarged through prayer."

Her lessons were simple but profound. Her teaching style was casual and conversational. One student testified, "She was well educated. She knew her subject and taught it well. She had a commanding presence; she was magnetic . . . You were drawn to her."

"Why," Mina asks her students, "is prayer often the last resort rather than the first thought? Prayer is our point of contact with God and our acknowledged dependence on him. Prayer is our admission that we cannot do without

God and our confession that there is a person greater, a power mightier, a force stronger, and a mind wiser than ourselves."

Prayer produces something special in a believer. "Prayer gives power as needed, a strength in weakness. It quiets the restless spirit, gives confidence, brings peace, and enlarges our spiritual vision. Prayer accomplishes the impossible!" For Mina, the key principle of prayer is knowing "that God is real, and he really cares about us."

After nineteen years at the College for Officer Training, Mina was transferred to territorial headquarters as the social welfare secretary. This was a shock and personal disappointment. "I was sure I was meant to remain on the college staff. I haven't always been in 100 percent agreement with my appointments, but I can wait!"

Again, a disappointment would become a blessing. In this appointment Mina not only remained on the Brengle Institute staff, but now she was free to travel the world, teaching the doctrine of holiness and the principles of prayer. "Sometimes, as I traveled to small and frightening places, I would just pray, 'Lord, thanks so much for letting my dreams come true, and thanks for taking care of me.' I felt protected and privileged."

Mina had one more appointment change before retirement. "Just as I felt I knew a little bit about the appointment as social-work secretary, I was moved on. Somebody said I was being moved because they had to make room for a man."

Has The Salvation Army diminished the role of the woman officer since the days of Catherine Booth?

"I think it has diminished, but I think women have often done it to themselves. The temptation in the Army is to be less than you can be. Sometimes, after being hurt, people decide to stay in the Army, but then they stay in and do less and are less of a person. Also, women's roles and positions have diminished because there is a preference for married couples."

On June 24, 1966, Brigadier Mina Russell retired from active service as an officer, but her activities did not end! She continued on the staff of the Brengle Institute until 1982, kindling holy fires within the lives of another generation of officers. During the years from 1966 until 1982, she took the light of the Holy Spirit and the power of prayer around the world. The sun never sets on the lives impacted by her teaching ministry.

At ninety-four years of age, hard of hearing and with failing eyesight, Mina says, "I've retired now. With my hearing and poor eyes, there isn't much I can do. . . . My responsibility now is to *be*. To be the person God wants me to be, to grow spiritually. I see this development in myself, and that feels very large. I continue to grow in faith. I am discovering how God takes care of little things, and I've discovered some things about wisdom and compassion. I have more time for prayer, and I'm learning to use my time to be what God wants me to *be*, not to *do*. Once I taught and traveled to spread the light of truth and holiness. Now I just let that light shine in me."

EPILOGUE

The Continuing Witness of Abandoned Love

While women weep, as they do now, I'll fight;
While little children go hungry, I'll fight;
While men go to prison, in and out, in and out,
    as they do now, I'll fight;
While there is a poor lost girl upon the streets,
Where there remains one dark soul without
    the light of God, I'll fight;
I'll fight to the very end!

—*William Booth*

With the interviews completed and hours of writing over, I noticed common threads running through the lives of these women whose ministries of love created such a lovely fragrance. Each of these female saints had a deeply committed personal relationship with God. From that relationship flowed an assurance of herself, knowing that God had created her to be exactly who she was, with her strengths and limitations. Knowing God and knowing herself, each came to understand God's purposes for her life. Then each woman allowed God to set the stage for the use of her gifts in leadership and ministry. These women were confident, focused, and purpose driven, all the while being spiritually sensitive and emotionally tender.

Some of them were called to perform heroic deeds while others were called to the more mundane. Some functioned in the public arena while others served in quieter, more private spheres of influence. A few women were mavericks, challenging the status quo, but most were called to live within a structured system. Although each is uniquely herself, all were called to godliness and service; all were called to sacrifice themselves for God. Each life is an example of the pouring out of self for the kingdom of God. Not striving for success, each has been successful because each woman has fulfilled God's plan through her life, thus influencing the world around her.

Catherine Booth, in her book, *Aggressive Christianity*, wrote of the success of the early disciples. She determined they succeeded in their mission because they gave wholehearted devotion to the mission; they each possessed an all-encompassing love for Christ; and they utterly renounced the things of the world in place of a heavenly treasure. She said, "Show the world a real, living, self-sacrificing, hard-working, toiling, triumphant Christianity, and the world will be influenced by it."

Whether that triumphant Christianity involves breaking an alabaster jar by preaching a sermon, caring for a family, singing a song, writing a poem, visiting the sick and imprisoned, or ministering to the needs of the homeless, the fragrance of abandoned love has always had an influence.

Joni Eareckson Tada was selected by the President of the United States to serve on the National Council on Disability. This appointment led to a thorough investigation into her personal life, and, when finally cleared, she had to be fingerprinted. The FBI agent had great difficulty getting prints from Joni's flaccid hands, which hadn't worked properly in over twenty years because of a diving accident that left her paralyzed. Finally, after trying four or five times, he gave up and said, "Lady, I'm sorry, but you just don't have any tread on those fingers of yours."

Joni's fingers were smooth, typical of those who can't or don't use their hands. The whirls and swirls on our fingers, defining our uniqueness, are deepened with use. Work enhances our prints.

Most people I know want to make some imprint on their world. Few will be famous, but all can make an imprint . . . at least in one other person's life. But to have that impact we have to get involved in life; we have to look to God for his purposes for us; and then we must forge ahead in faith. We will face difficulties and challenges, but we must stay committed to the pouring out of ourselves in service and ministry. Each of us needs to do what we can.

Every person is a divine original. On planet Earth, with over five billion people, each person is a one-of-a-kind miracle. Dare to be God's miracle, filling your world with the fragrance of his love and grace. Who knows, maybe only you can touch a certain person or accomplish a specific task.

Esther was the young and beautiful queen of King Xerxes, whose kingdom stretched from the upper Nile River to India. Esther, a Jew, had miraculously been raised from the slave status of her people and now lived in the luxury of the palace. Watching her people suffer under bondage, she found herself in a place of influence. Having access to power, she might be able to ease their distress.

Mordecai, her cousin, challenged Esther to take advantage of the place God had put her and the skills he had given her. The proposed action brought great personal risk to Esther, but Mordecai was unrelenting. He moved Esther into action with these words: "And who knows but that you have come to the kingdom for such a time as this?" (Esther 4:14).

It was Esther's time! In less than a week the lives of the Jewish people were spared by one woman's willingness to risk by an act of abandoned love. The annual feast of Purim marks this important event in Jewish history.

I wonder—looking at the sphere of influence that surrounds you, knowing that God has placed you where you are, with the gifts, strengths, and limitations that make you unique—have you come to the kingdom for such a time as this?

What opportunities has God placed before you that require a breaking of self will and an abandoned pouring out of love? What prints does God want you to make on your world? What risk can you take that will permeate the world with the fragrance of God's love, mercy, and grace?

Women have been faithful in the past. Can we be anything less today? The continuing witness of female servants in the kingdom of God is not only a statement of spiritual freedom, it is a demonstration of the courage of women throughout history who ran their race, carried their torch, and passed it on to the next generation. Commissioner Kay

F. Rader said, "We [women] have been pacesetters in the past. We want to keep faith with that heritage."

President Bill Clinton, speaking at the fiftieth anniversary of D-day, which commemorated the end of World War II, said, "We are the children of your sacrifice." As a woman in Christian ministry, ordained for leadership in the church, I am the child of previous generations of self-sacrificing women and progressive-thinking men. Through the actions of my life and those in my generation, what will be passed on to my children and grandchildren?

Scripture is clear, "There is neither Jew nor Greek, slave nor free, male nor female, for you are all one in Christ Jesus" (Galatians 3:28).

The Salvation Army, through the insight and courage of Catherine Booth, unbolted a door of ministry for women of the world to walk through. Revelation 3:8 says, "See, I have placed before you an open door." Speaking of this verse, Catherine said, "When God gives the inward urging, he opens the outward door. When he qualifies a person for work, he opens a way to that work."

Take courage, break your alabaster jar, and do something wonderfully significant for Jesus!

BIBLIOGRAPHY

The interviews in this book are of two natures: fiction and nonfiction. The women of past history, profiled in the first part of each chapter, are fictional interviews. After researching each woman, her ministry, and her culture, knowing what could be known I conducted a fictitious interview, hopefully not just a figment of my imagination but one that captured the woman and her heart. The women making current history and still living, profiled in the second part of each chapter, did in fact tell me their stories. As much as possible, their own words were used.

Years of reading laid the foundation for information and views represented in this book. The following are some of the resources used:

Aburdene, Patricia, and John Naisbitt. *Megatrends for Women.* New York: Villard Books, 1992.

Adeney, Miriam. *A Time for Risking: Priorities for Women.* Portland: Multnomah Press, 1987.

Armistead, Norman. *For God Alone: Devotional Thoughts from the Writings of Catherine Booth.* Belfast: Ambassador Productions Ltd., 1990.

Bainton, Roland H. *The Reformation of the Sixteenth Century.* Boston: Beacon Press, 1952.

Baird, Catherine. *Book of Salvationist Verse.* St. Albans: The Camfield Press, 1963.

Barnes, Cyril. *God's Army.* London: Lion Publishing, 1978.

———. *With Booth in London.* St. Albans: The Campfield Press, 1986.

———. *Words of Catherine Booth.* St. Albans: The Campfield Press, 1981.

———. *Words of William Booth.* St. Albans: The Campfield Press.

Booth, Catherine. *Aggressive Christianity: Practical Sermons.* Boston: McDonald & Gill, 1883.

———. *"Female Ministry: Or Woman's Right to Preach the Gospel."* London: 1859.

Bramwell-Booth, Catherine, and Catherine Booth. *The Story of Her Loves.* London: Hodder and Stoughton, 1970.

Booth, Evangeline. *Woman.* New York: Fleming Y. Revell Company, 1930.

Bowie, Fiona, and Oliver Davies. *Hildegard of Bingen: Mystical Writings.* New York: The Crossroad Publishing Company, 1993.

Temple Bristow, John. *What Paul Really Said about Women*. San Francisco: Harper & Row, Publishers, 1988.

McNall Burns, Edward, Robert E. Lerner and Standish Meacham. *Western Civilizations: Their History and Their Culture*, vol. 1, 9th ed. New York: W.W. Norton & Company, 1980.

Carmichael, Amy. *If*. London: SPCK Publishers, 1938.

Chesham, Sallie. *Born to Battle: The Salvation Army in America*. San Francisco: Rand McNally and Company, 1965.

Coutts, Frederick. *No Discharge in This War: A One Volume History of The Salvation Army*. London: Hodder and Stoughton, 1974.

————. *The Better Fight: The History of The Salvation Army, vol. 6. 1914–1946*, London: Hodder and Stoughton, 1973.

Dargatz, Jan. *Women & Power*. Vancouver: Thomas Nelson Publishers, 1995.

Deen, Edith. *All the Women of the Bible*. New York: Harper & Row, Publishers, Inc., 1955.

————. *Great Women of the Christian Faith*. Uhrichsville: Barbour and Company, Inc., 1959.

Hoadley Dick, Lois, and Amy Carmichael. *Let the Little Children Come*. Chicago: Moody Press, 1984.

Douglas, J. D. *Encyclopedia of Religious Knowledge*. 2d ed., Grand Rapids: Baker Book House, 1991.

Elliot, Elizabeth. *A Chance to Die: The Life and Legacy of Amy Carmichael*. Grand Rapids: Fleming H. Revell, 1987.

Elwell, Walter A. *Baker Encyclopedia of the Bible*, vol. 1. Grand Rapids: Baker Book House, 1988.

———. *Baker Encyclopedia of the Bible*, vol. 2. Grand Rapids: Baker Book House, 1988.

———. *Evangelical Dictionary of Theology*. Grand Rapids: Baker Book House, 1984.

Evans, Mary J. *Woman in the Bible: An Overview of All the Crucial Passages on Women's Roles*. Downers Grove: InterVarsity Press, 1983.

Fairbank, Jenty. *William and Catherine Booth: God's Soldiers*. London: Hodder and Stoughton, 1974.

Green, Roger. *Catherine Booth: A Biography of the Cofounder of The Salvation Army*. Grand Rapids: Baker Books, 1996.

Merrill Groothuis, Rebecca. *Women Caught in the Conflict: The Culture War between Traditionalism and Feminism*. Grand Rapids: Baker Books, 1994.

Hayford, Jack W., with Wendy Parrish. *Biblical Ministries through Women: God's Daughters and God's Work*. Nashville: Thomas Nelson Publishers, 1994.

Heine, Susanne. *Women and Early Christianity: A Reappraisal*. Minneapolis: Augsburg Publishing House, 1988.

Hollister, C. Warren. *Medieval Europe: A Short History*. 5th ed., New York: Alfred A. Knopf, 1982.

Jewett, Paul K. *The Ordination of Women: An Essay on the Office of Christian Ministry*. Grand Rapids: William B. Eerdmans Publishing Company, 1980.

Kew, Clifford W. *Catherine Booth: Her Continuing Relevance*. St. Albans: The Campfield Press, 1990.

Clark Kroeger, Catherine and Richard Clark Kroeger. *I Suffer Not a Woman: Rethinking I Timothy 2:11–15 in Light of Ancient Evidence*. Grand Rapids: Baker Book House, 1992.

Larsson, Flora. *My Best Men Are Women*, London: Hodder and Stoughton, 1974.

Latourette, Kenneth Scott. *A History of Christianity: Beginnings to 1500*, vol. 1. San Francisco: HarperCollins Publishers, 1975.

———. *A History of Christianity: Reformation to the Present*, vol. 2. San Francisco: HarperCollins Publishers, 1975.

Ludwig, Charles. *Mother of an Army*. Minneapolis: Bethany House Publishers, 1987.

MacHaffie, Barbara J. *Her Story: Women in Christian Tradition*. Minneapolis: Fortress Press, 1986.

———. *Readings in Her Story: Women in Christian Tradition*. Minneapolis: Fortress Press, 1992.

Torjesen Malcolm, Kari. *Women at the Crossroads*. Downers Grove: InterVarsity Press, 1982.

Mickelsen, Alvera. *Women, Authority and the Bible*. Downers Grove: InterVarsity Press, 1986.

Ramey Mollenkott, Virginia. *Women, Men and the Bible*. New York: The Crossroad Publishing Company, 1988.

Murdoch, Norman H. *Origins of The Salvation Army*. Knoxville: The University of Tennessee Press, 1994.

Price, Eugenia. *The Unique World of Women . . . in Bible Times and Now*. Grand Rapids: Zondervan Publishing House, 1969.

Rhemick, John R. *A New People of God: A Study in Salvationism*. Des Plaines: The Salvation Army Central Territory, 1993.

Radford Ruether, Rosemary, and Rosemary Skinner Keller. *Women & Religion in America*, vol. 3, 1900–1968. San Francisco: Harper & Row, Publishers, 1986.

Reid, Daniel G., Robert D. Linder, Bruce L. Shelley, and Harry S. Stout, *Dictionary of Christianity in America*. Downers Grove: InterVarsity Press, 1990.

Roe, Earl O. *Dream Big: The Henrietta Mears Story*. Ventura: Regal Books, 1990.

Sandall, Robert. *The History of The Salvation Army*, vol. 1, 1865–1878. London: Thomas Nelson and Sons Ltd., 1947.

————. *The History of The Salvation Army*, vol. 2, 1878–1886. London: Thomas Nelson and Sons Ltd., 1950.

Satterlee, Allen. *Notable Quotables: A Compendium of Gems from Salvation Army Literature*. Atlanta: The Salvation Army Southern Territory, 1985.

Shelley, Bruce L. *Church History in Plain Language*. Waco: Word Books Publisher, 1982.

Skoglund, Elizabeth R. *AMMA: The Life and Words of Amy Carmichael*. Grand Rapids: Baker Books, 1994.

Stead, W. T. *General Booth: A Biographical Sketch*. London: Isbister and Company Limited, 1891.

————. *Mrs. Booth of The Salvation Army*. London: James Nisbet & Co. Limited, 1900.

Torjesen, Karen Jo. *When Women Were Priests*. San Francisco: HarperCollins Publishers, 1993.

Trible, Phyllis. *Texts of Terror*. Philadelphia: Fortress Press, 1984.

Tucker, Ruth A., and Walter Liefeld. *Daughters of the Church: Women and Ministry from New Testament Times to the Present*. Grand Rapids: Academie Books of Zondervan Publishing House, 1987.

Tucker, Ruth A. *Women in the Maze: Questions & Answers on Biblical Equality*. Downers Grove: InterVarsity Press, 1992.

Waldron, John D. *The Quakers and the Salvationists*. Atlanta: The Salvation Army Southern Territory, 1990.

———. *Women in The Salvation Army*. Oakville, Ontario: The Triumph Press, 1983.

Watson, Bernard. *A Hundred Years' War*. London: Hodder and Stoughton Ltd., 1964.

Wiggins, Arch. *The History of the Salvation Army*, vol. 5, 1886–1904. London: Thomas Nelson and Sons Ltd., 1964.

Christian History Magazine: Issue 17, Issue 26, Issue 28, Issue 31, Issue 34, Issue 36, Issue 37, Issue 39, Issue 47, Issue 49, Issue 52.

The Salvation Army: Its Origin and Development. Issued by authority of the General. London: Salvationist Publishing and Supplies, Limited, 1927.

They Said It: William and Catherine Booth, St. Albans: The Campfield Press, 1978.